Faces of African Independence
Three Plays

12.95

Faces of
African Independence

THREE PLAYS

Three Suitors: One Husband
and
Until Further Notice

By Guillaume Oyônô-Mbia

The Death of Chaka

by Seydou Badian

translated by Clive Wake

Introduction by Richard Bjornson

CARAF BOOKS

University Press of Virginia

CHARLOTTESVILLE

This is a title in the CARAF BOOKS series

Three Suitors: One Husband, originally published in French
as *Trois Prétendants: Un Mari* by Editions CLE, Cameroun in 1964,
was first published in this English language version in 1968
by Methuen and Co., Ltd., 11 New Fetter Lane, London EC4.
English version Copyright © 1968 by Guillaume Oyônô-Mbia

Until Further Notice first published 1968
Copyright © 1968 by Guillaume Oyônô-Mbia
Reprinted 1974 and 1978 by Eyre Methuen

La Mort de Chaka Copyright © Présence Africaine, Paris, 1962.
English translation—*The Death of Chaka*—Copyright
© Oxford University Press, Nairobi, 1968.
This edition
published in agreement with Présence Africaine
and Oxford University Press, Nairobi, 1986.

This English-language edition is available for sale
only in the United States of America.

UNIVERSITY PRESS OF VIRGINIA

Introduction to this volume
Copyright © 1988 by the Rector and Visitors
of the University of Virginia

Second paperback printing 1990

Library of Congress Cataloging-in-Publication Data

Faces of African independence : three plays / translated by Clive Wake ;
introduction by Richard Bjornson.
p.   cm. — (CARAF books)
Contents: Three suitors, one husband / by Guillaume Oyônô-Mbia —
Until further notice / by Guillaume Oyônô Mbia — The death of Chaka /
by Seydou Badian.
ISBN 0-8139-1186-9.   ISBN 0-8139-1187-7 (pbk.)
1. African drama (French)—20th century—Translations into
English.   2. English drama—Translations from French.   3. Africa—
History—Autonomy and independence movements—Drama.   4. Chaka,
Zulu Chief, 1787?–1828—Drama.   5. Oyônô-Mbia, Guillaume, 1939– —
Translations, English.   I. Oyônô-Mbia, Guillaume, 1939–   Trois
prétendants, un mari. English. 1988.   II. Oyônô-Mbia, Guillaume,
1939–   Until further notice. 1988.   III. Badian, Seydou, 1928–
Mort de Chaka. English. 1988.   IV. Series.
PQ3987.5.E5F33   1988   842—dc19   88-6976   CIP

Printed in the United States of America

Contents

Introduction

As the colonial period drew to a close in most of French-speaking Africa during the late 1950s and early 1960s, a new theater began to emerge. At first it consisted largely of little-known plays written for local production by amateur troupes. There were also a certain number of literary dramas published in France and intended for reading as well as for acting. Guillaume Oyônô-Mbia's *Three Suitors: One Husband* is of the first sort; it was written in 1959 while the author was still a student at the American Presbyterian mission school, Libamba, in south-central Cameroon, and it was first staged by his young classmates. Seydou Badian's *Death of Chaka* is the second sort of play. A medical doctor who had studied at the University of Montpellier (France) before becoming Minister of Rural Development and Planning in Mali when that country became independent in 1960, he recast the story of the powerful early nineteenth-century Zulu leader Chaka to raise the consciousness of contemporary Africans with regard to the need for discipline and creative leadership in the nation-building process that was confronting most of them at that time. As a result, his *Death of Chaka*, published in Paris in 1962, lends itself to being read as an ideological problem play, whereas Oyônô-Mbia's dramas achieve their greatest impact when they are staged as entertainments. That is not to say that *Three Suitors: One Husband* lacks serious social commentary or that *The Death of Chaka* is inappropriate for the stage, but they do represent opposite poles in the spectrum of early francophone African theater.

Introduction

Of all the conventional European literary genres, drama is perhaps best suited for adaptation to the African situation. After all, there are numerous theatrical elements in traditional African life: oral storytellers accompany their tales with gestures and mimicry, initiation rituals include dramatizations of important moral truths, and other rites demand various kinds of acting ability. Furthermore, in societies where up to 85 percent of the people are illiterate or semiliterate, the potential audience for oral forms of literary expression is larger than for written ones. Nevertheless, there is a major obstacle to the success of the theater in French-speaking Africa, and it involves the choice of the language. Most writers from this part of the continent have received their education in European-style schools; they speak French fluently, but the majority of their compatriots feel more at home in an African language. Since the official language in these countries is French, there are more opportunities to produce French-language plays than African-language ones. Writers themselves generally desire to communicate with a larger audience than they could ever reach if they wrote in a language that can only be understood by a relatively small number of people.

Furthermore, the French government has contributed enormously to the continued use of French as a primary language of cultural expression in its former colonies. The cultural affairs office has generously subsidized touring French theatrical troupes and has sponsored training sessions for African actors, and the French National Radio conducts an annual drama competition that has attracted thousands of entries. A relatively large number of these plays is selected for broadcast to Africa. The significance of this contest is illustrated by the fact that far more than half the plays produced in the former French colonies since its inception in 1967 were initially submitted to this competition. For a variety of reasons, then, most of the drama from these countries continues to be written in French and influenced by French theatrical conventions. Thus, although some plays like *Three Suitors: One Husband* have proved immensely popular in Africa, the potential of the

Introduction

theater as a universally accessible literary genre has not yet been fully realized in the former French colonies. With the notable exception of experiments by dramatists like Bernard Zadi Zaourou from the Ivory Coast and Werewere Liking from Cameroon, most francophone African plays remain hybrid forms that appeal largely to the educated minorities in these countries.

Despite the theatrical elements in traditional African life, theater as such did not exist in the French colonies until young Africans began to adapt their own customs, dances, and social practices for presentation as European-style performances. It is in this sense that francophone African drama is a hybrid phenomenon, for if the subject matter is unmistakably African, the language and form have always been strongly influenced by European precedent. The earliest experiments along these lines took place in the William Ponty School on the island of Gorée in Senegal during the 1930s. Drawn from all over French West Africa, the elite students at William Ponty collected material from their own ethnic groups and incorporated it into end-of-the-year performances. These performances proved highly successful, and the students toured major cities in the region with their productions. In 1937, they even performed at the Théâtre des Champs Elysées in Paris.

The subject matter of the Ponty productions tended to be assimilationist in the sense that they presented traditional customs and subject matter from the vantage point of Africans who accepted European culture as their standard of value. Nevertheless, these plays established a precedent for African dramatic writing in French, and they stimulated the interest of several young men who later contributed significantly to the emergence of African theater in the former French colonies. Bernard Dadié came from the Ivory Coast, and he wrote the play that was produced in Paris. He later became the best-known francophone African playwright; his *Béatrice du Congo* (1971) and *Monsieur Thôgô-Gnini* (1970) continue to be performed throughout the continent. Fodeba Keita from Guinea also produced plays for the Ponty group, and he later founded the highly successful "Ballets Africains." Despite the impact of the Ponty experience, however, a theater that reflected genuinely African preoccupations did not arise until about the time of independence (ca. 1960).

. Both Oyônô-Mbia and Badian were important figures in this development. By humorously depicting a controversy over bride-price in a small Cameroonian village, Oyônô-Mbia reveals the underlying conflicts that afflict contemporary African society—conflicts between generations, conflicts between traditional and modern systems of value, conflicts between honesty and corruption. Badian's more serious approach to the Chaka theme enables him to demonstrate that Africans have a history of which they can be proud (an important consideration in the aftermath of colonialist denigration of all African values). At the same time, he uses the example of Chaka to illustrate the attitudes he regards as necessary if Africans are to succeed in forging new nations grounded in self-respect and freedom. The plays in this volume thus reflect two different approaches to African reality at the dawn of independence. They differ from the earlier Ponty performances insofar as they express a concern for reality as perceived from a genuinely African perspective. In this sense, they helped launch a francophone African-theater tradition that has continued to grow and expand during the past thirty years.

One of the most brilliantly talented writers to emerge from the Bulu country in south-central Cameroon, Oyônô-Mbia is well-known as a raconteur of humorous anecdotes in French and in Bulu. He himself fondly recalls the tales he heard as a child, and the worldview imbedded in these tales resurfaces in the form of the plays he has written: *Three Suitors: One Husband, Until Further Notice, His Excellency's Special Train,* and *Our Daughter Shall Not Marry.* One of the most popular characters in the Bulu oral tradition is Kulu the tortoise, who often prevails over physically stronger creatures through the use of clever stratagems. Two of the most common moral observations associated with the Kulu tales involve (1) the recog-

Introduction

nition that superior force always prevails in a harsh world where being right does not guarantee survival and (2) the realization that physically stronger creatures can be dominated by weaker ones if they allow themselves to be blinded by pride, gullibility, or the single-minded pursuit of a narrowly defined goal. In these tales, the dupes of Kulu's ruses are presented as objects of laughter, thereby reinforcing the assumption that force is, in part, a function of one's intellectual perceptiveness. Similarly, all of Oyônô-Mbia's plays are based upon the wry acceptance of a harsh reality that assures neither progress toward a better future, nor the ultimate triumph of justice. In the fictional worlds he has created, people blinded by pride, gullibility, or some obsessive preoccupation often make foolish mistakes and allow themselves to be duped by others.

Yet Oyônô-Mbia is also fully aware of the changes that have taken place since the days when animal tales could convey all the wisdom necessary for coping with a self-contained ethnic society and the surrounding natural world. In fact, much of the comedy in his plays arises from the fact that, although people's values have changed, they insist upon retaining beliefs and modes of behavior that are incompatible with their new values. For example, the principal new values in contemporary African society are money and the prestige associated with it. The desire for money often blinds people to the truth about themselves and others. It also causes them to pursue wealth and status with the utmost seriousness. To reveal the absurdity of this seriousness in a harsh world where everyone must eventually die, Oyônô-Mbia invents actions that resemble a game in which the audience is invited to participate. The purpose of this game is twofold: it serves a socially critical function by ripping the veil of respectability from attitudes that also exist in the everyday world of the spectators, and it suggests that the celebratory sense of life (in which three of his four plays culminate) is a redemptive quality for people condemned to live in a world governed by forces beyond their control. These plays are entertainments. They provoke laugh-

Introduction

ter. Yet when spectators reflect on the causes of their laughter, they recognize that Oyônô-Mbia is also commenting provocatively upon the nature of existence in contemporary Africa.

Three Suitors: One Husband was written shortly before Cameroonian independence. After having visited his village during a school vacation, Oyônô-Mbia returned to Libamba and told his friends about the palaver that had taken place on the subject of his cousin's marriage. When he started to write down the anecdote for his own amusement, a young French teacher encouraged him to transform it into a play. Although Oyônô-Mbia claims never to have seen an actual theatrical production before *Three Suitors: One Husband* was staged at Libamba the following year, he was familiar with the dramatic techniques of traditional storytellers, and he had seen religious skits staged at the mission churches during Easter and Christmas. In addition, he had read and admired the plays of Molière. From all these experiences, he conceived the idea that plays and stories should entertain people, while criticizing their foibles and revealing truths they might have overlooked in their own experience of everyday reality. At the same time, he enjoyed playing with words and evoking situations that would make people laugh.

The first production of *Three Suitors: One Husband* was so successful that the students at Libamba brought it to the Cameroonian capital, Yaoundé, where they performed it before enthusiastic audiences at the French Cultural Center in 1961. By 1964 Oyônô-Mbia had made several trips to France and participated in a conference on African drama. Thus, when he directed the play at Libamba in the spring of that year, he introduced several changes in the text, and these were incorporated into the first published version that appeared at that time. During the next five years, Oyônô-Mbia attended the University of Keele in England, where he himself translated it for a student production in 1967. As a result of his continued work on the play, he modified the second French edition of his text when he returned to Cameroon in 1969, and this version has generally been accepted as the standard text of the play.

The action in *Three Suitors: One Husband* is relatively simple. It revolves around a conflict of values and a conflict of generations. After having paid for the young woman Juliette's schooling at Libamba, her father, Atangana, and the elders of Mvoutessi expect her to marry whomever they choose. Basically they anticipate a handsome return on their investment in her education, because they would all receive a share of the bride-price and the countless other presents her fiancé would presumably offer them. However, Juliette herself has fallen in love with a fellow student, Oko, and she refuses to acquiesce in their plans. Atangana had initially accepted a 100,000 CFA franc bride-price from the young farmer Ndi, but when the polygamous civil servant Mbia offers him 200,000 CFA francs, he takes it as well.[1] Upon the arrival of Oko, Juliette steals the entire 300,000 francs and gives them to him. When Atangana discovers the theft, he tries to extort additional payments from Ndi to reimburse Mbia and from Mbia to reimburse Ndi, but both of them threaten reprisals for Atangana's alleged breach of contract, and the village elders have recourse to a sorcerer in hopes of recovering the lost money. His mystifying charade proves futile, and, exasperated by his greed, they chase the sorcerer from Mvoutessi and seek to convince the Bamileke merchant Tchetgen to give them a sufficiently large dowry to pay back the first two suitors.[2] At this point, Oko reappears. Dressed ostentatiously as an important personage, he feigns resistance to their sugges-

---

[1] Fifty CFA francs are the equivalent of one French franc. At the time the play was written the American dollar was worth approximately five French francs; therefore, Ndi's dowry payment of 100,000 CFA francs amounted to approximately $400, far more than the annual income of the average Cameroonian.

[2] In Cameroon the Bamileke are commonly known and often resented for their entrepreneurial skills and acquisitiveness, somewhat like the Ibo in Nigeria.

tions that he marry Juliette. Before relenting, he insists that she herself agree to the marriage. When she does, he presents the stolen 300,000 francs to Atangana, and the play ends as the audience is invited to participate in an outburst of singing and dancing on the stage.

The immediate impact of *Three Suitors: One Husband* is that of comedy. People laugh at the naive self-importance, the ignorance, and the avidity of the villagers; at the pretentiousness of the civil servant Mbia; at the miserliness of the merchant Tchetgen; and at malapropisms, puns, and humorous misunderstandings in the text. Cameroonians have no difficulty in recognizing the skill with which Oyônô-Mbia has captured representative features of characters, speech patterns, and situations with which they are familiar in their day-to-day lives, and younger spectators, like those who watched the first performance of the play at Libamba, delight in the ruse that enables Juliette and Oko to circumvent the plans of her father and the other villagers. Indeed, the ending of the play constitutes a celebration of life and suggests the possibility of a momentary reconciliation of competing interests. Yet, despite its essentially comic thrust, Oyônô-Mbia's drama reflects the existence of a social malaise that is never completely resolved.

For example, the European colonization of Africa introduced changes that deeply affected the life in villages like Mvoutessi, and although people sought to accommodate these changes within traditional institutions, the resultant contradictions were so great that the society itself acquired a number of grotesquely comic features. In Bulu society, for example, marriage was traditionally viewed as an alliance between the two families. In this context, the bride-price usually involved the gift of local produce, domestic animals, or the work needed to build a house or clear a field. It was intended to symbolically recompense the woman's family for expenses incurred in raising a child whose labor and fertility would later contribute to the wealth of her husband's family. With

Introduction

the introduction of European-style schooling and a money economy, the bride-price acquired an entirely different character. When a girl like Juliette was sent to school, her parents often could not afford to pay her fees. As a result, other members of her family and other villagers were called upon to contribute. Because her schooling would make her eligible to marry a man of a higher social rank, the villagers expected to be repaid in the form of a higher bride-price. However, the demand for money rather than in-kind contributions transformed the nature of the transaction. From a symbolic exchange that cemented the alliance of two families, it evolved into a cash transaction, reducing the young woman to a commodity that could be bought and sold.

Ironically, the very process of attending school exposed younger people like Juliette to European ideas of individual freedom and romantic love. As the bride-price became increasingly linked with monetary payments, many older men began to regard their daughters as potential sources of wealth. Such a situation militated against younger men, who usually lacked the financial resources to meet demands for exorbitant bride-prices. At the same time, it favored older men who could easily "purchase" younger wives. Under such circumstances, generational conflict is inevitable, for as older men defend their prerogative to marry younger women and to profit from their own daughters' marriages, younger women increasingly desire to choose their own partners, whereas younger men become more outspoken in proclaiming their right to marry, even when they are unable to compete financially with their elders. This conflict stands at the center of *Three Suitors: One Husband.*

It is not exactly a conflict between traditional and modern values, for the traditions according to which Atangana and the elders justify their decisions have been adulterated by a characteristically European pursuit of economic self-interest. Contrasting with the spontaneous laughter and celebratory attitude that surfaces in all of Oyônô-Mbia's plays, this sort of calculation brings about the malaise that afflicts the larger world of which Mvoutessi is a small part—a malaise that persists even in the background of the play's happy ending. At a point when nearly everyone is seeking to convince Juliette that she should marry the civil servant Mbia, she asks if money is proof of love. In contrast to the answer she anticipates, the older women in the village assure her that the size of the bride-price a man is willing to pay does reflect the intensity of his love, and her cousin Matalina cannot understand why any woman would hesitate to marry a wealthy man who can provide her with fine clothes, a villa in town, and an automobile. Their unexpected replies to her rhetorical question are based on the assumption that marriage is like a business deal in which the woman receives prestige and material possessions in return for her sexual favors. In their opinion, Juliette should be happy if her family can conclude an advantageous deal with Mbia on her behalf.

Furthermore, each of the villagers hopes to receive some personal benefit from the transaction. The money that Atangana had spent for Juliette's education could have been used for other purposes—to acquire an additional wife for himself, to send one of the other children to school, or to provide the bride-price that would allow one of his sons to marry. In preference to such alternative uses, he had invested it in her education, and like the others who had contributed from their cocoa earnings, he regarded the money offered by Ndi and Mbia as a legitimate profit on his investment. Because he wanted to maximize this profit, he preferred Mbia's higher offer and the implicit promise of supplementary benefits like gun permits, medals, cases of alcoholic beverages, and visits to the city. Other inhabitants of Mvoutessi also saw how their own interests might be served by Juliette's marriage to a prestigious civil servant. Her grandfather Abessolo expected to receive cloth and kola nuts; her brother Oyônô anticipated money to pay the bride-price for the woman he wanted to marry; her uncle Ondua envisaged an exemption from police harrassment for his well-known drunkenness and his wife's il-

Introduction

legal *arki* distillery;[3] Matalina dreams of having relatives with whom she can stay in the city. All these wishes are variations upon the theme of self-interest; each person wants something for himself or herself.

The most exaggerated examples of self-interest are embodied in the characters of the pretentious Mbia, the sorcerer Sanga-Tita (who repeatedly interrupts his burlesque incantations to demand additional payments), and the Bamileke merchant Tchetgen, but the same tendency is present in most of the villagers, who are quite willing to sell Juliette to the highest bidder as long as their own desires are satisfied. After the loss of the 300,000 francs, which must be repaid to Ndi and Mbia, the village chief, Mbarga, goes so far as to suggest that Atangana could parade his daughter in front of all the ministers in Yaoundé and then give her to anyone who offered to pay at least that much for her.

Although Mbarga's suggestion is a logical extension of the villagers' attitude toward Juliette's marriage, it reveals the extent to which she has become a saleable object in their eyes. She herself objects to this proceeding because she sees herself in completely different terms. In fact, much of the play's dramatic tension derives from the opposition between her conception of herself and the others' conception of what her role ought to be in the business transaction called marriage. Abessolo and Atangana assume that Juliette will have nothing to say about her own marriage, for according to traditional custom, daughters should unquestioningly obey the commands of their fathers and village elders. Furthermore, Abessolo reminds her that she has an obligation to repay the expenses they incurred in sending her to "Dibamba" (a humorous deformation of Libamba, the actual school where Oyônô-Mbia first staged the play) and a duty to provide the bride-price for her brother's marriage. In his eyes, schooling

---

[3] *Arki* is a grain alcohol that the villagers in south-central Cameroon distill for local consumption, despite its prohibition by government authorities.

and European ideas have corrupted Juliette and rendered her disobedient. He even suggests that disobedient daughters should, like disobedient wives, be beaten until they conform to traditional mores.

His outrage at the younger generation's lack of respect for customary practices is humorously illustrated by a comic misunderstanding that arises after Atangana discovers the theft of the 300,000 francs and announces that "they" have left nothing behind. He means the thieves, of course, but the older men think he is referring to several young men who recently killed a viper and left none of the meat for them, in blatant disregard of the taboo that ordains that only older men are allowed to eat such delicacies. The substitution of the viper for the money symbolically suggests the way older men in Bulu society reserve certain privileges for themselves and seek to retain these privileges even when society changes dramatically, as it had changed with the introduction of a money economy.

Atangana himself has planted an enormous alarm clock in front of him in the opening scene of the play, because he wants to make certain that his wife, Makrita, returns from the fields by noon in order to prepare his dinner. His insistence upon absolute obedience is based upon traditional social values, but his means of enforcing his desire is borrowed from European concepts of time. He himself fails to realize that the values behind a single-minded pursuit of one's own economic self-interest and the assumption that time can be determined with mechanical precision are incompatible with the values that originally defined man-woman relationships and institutions like the bride-price in traditional society. Nevertheless, nearly all the villagers accept his interpretation of the situation as normal and natural. They are astonished that Juliette would think otherwise.

However, her idea that marriage should be based upon love and the freedom to choose one's own partner merely reflects another dimension of the European value system that had already intruded into their own attitudes toward life. When she proclaims that she is a free human being with an intrinsic value of her own, she is adapting a modern concept of selfhood to her own personal situation. Oyônô-Mbia's characters frequently observe that the world is changing, but the villagers at Mvoutessi have not yet grasped all the ramifications of this change, and their naive response to it produces a comic effect; however, the ultimate triumph of Juliette and Oko suggests that the adulterated traditions of Atangana's generation represent a transitional stage in an evolution away from outmoded sensibilities and ways of thinking. Such changes are not always positive, but they are irreversible.

What is positive in Oyônô-Mbia's play is the laughter that frees individuals from the exaggerated seriousness with which they pursue their own self-interest. Positive too is a human capacity for experiencing the exuberance present in communal singing and dancing. In several interviews, Oyônô-Mbia has mentioned his belief that drama represents an opportunity to reach illiterate as well as literate audiences. One way to achieve this goal is to involve spectators in the laughter and celebration portrayed on the stage. Audiences laugh at the foibles of Oyônô-Mbia's characters, but the characters themselves also laugh, and the audiences laugh with them. This shared laughter is encouraged by the fact that the author introduces characters and situations in which African audiences could recognize a part of their own milieu. In the notes to several of his plays, he urges directors in other parts of Africa to enhance this sense of recognition by substituting local costumes and songs for the Bulu ones in his original text.

At the same time, Oyônô-Mbia continually reminds audiences that, like an oral story being told in a traditional setting, the play is an artificial creation. In *Three Suitors: One Husband,* for example, Oko and Juliette's cousin Kouma leave the scene at the end of act 2 after receiving the 300,000 francs from Juliette and announcing their intention to stage a performance that will impress the villagers with Oko's wealth and prestige. Kouma then turns to the audience and shouts, "See you in the fifth act . . .!" Such intentional breaks in the play's illusion of verisimilitude predispose spectators to regard the entire drama as a clever game in which they, too, are participants. Thus, although characters like Atangana, Abessolo, and Mbia display characteristics of real people, the emphasis upon their status as actors in a playfully construed fictional world enables the audience to gain a certain distance from them. This distancing in turn allows spectators to laugh at aspects of their own reality—aspects that people tend to regard as normal and natural when they encounter them in everyday life.

The idea of drama as a participatory game reaches its climax in the final scene when the entire audience is invited onto the stage to join in the singing and dancing that mark Juliette's engagement to Oko. At this point the spectators become actors. The fictional occasion for their participation is no longer of central importance, for by laughing and singing and dancing, they adopt the attitude that life can be a celebration, and that attitude is the best antidote against the pretentiousness and self-interested behavior they have witnessed on the stage and in real life. A socially critical play, *Three Suitors: One Husband* provokes insight by implicitly challenging people to reflect upon the reasons behind their own responses to the action. By inviting the people in the audience to drop their masks (as the actors had done) and to participate in an outburst of spontaneous joy that testifies to the humanity that they share with everyone around them, Oyônô-Mbia is seeking to produce a catharsis that presupposes a worldview similar to that expressed in traditional Bulu tales. Like them, his play places primary importance upon an ability to see through false appearances. At the same time, it reinforces the idea that laughter and the celebration of life can help make a harsh reality bearable. Oyônô-Mbia's comic vision is, however, not entirely traditional, for he clearly supports the individual freedom and romantic love that triumph in the final act of the play.

Until Further Notice is organized around similar themes and dramatic techniques. Originally written in English as a

---

Introduction

one-act radio play, it received first prize in a 1967 BBC drama contest. Oyônô-Mbia himself then translated it into French at the behest of a friend, the Cameroonian actor and director Ambroise M'bia. This script was recorded in 1967 for broadcast by the French National Radio Service and was then modified slightly for the stage presentation that M'bia directed later that year in Yaoundé. Because it was performed by the troupe that would later become the Cameroonian National Theater, many of the country's best-known actors appeared in it at that time. This stage version was published in 1970, and it has proved nearly as popular as *Three Suitors: One Husband*. Once again, the action takes place in Mvoutessi and revolves around the villagers' expectation that they will benefit materially from the marriage of a young woman whose educational costs they helped defray. Matalina had studied nursing in France, where she met and married a young doctor. Upon the couple's return to Cameroon, the newlyweds lived in Yaoundé for three months without coming to visit her family, because the doctor was awaiting his assignment to a hospital. He had initially desired to serve in the backcountry, where he thought he would be most useful to the greatest number of people, but the government offered him a prestigious administrative position in the capital, and the people of Mvoutessi want him to accept it, for they clearly hope to benefit from his status. On the day of the play's action, Matalina's father, Abessolo, and the other villagers await the announced visit of the young couple; however, when the doctor accepts the administrative position, he cancels their scheduled trip to Mvoutessi and sends a formal letter in which he regrets that they will be unable to come "until further notice." The letter is brought to Abessolo by the doctor's driver, who also presents the old man with many cases of beer, wine, and food. The villagers have already begun to dance at the news of the doctor's acceptance of the prestigious position, and Abessolo proudly announces that there will be festivities at his house that night. Like *Three Suitors: One Husband, Until Further Notice* reveals the calculated self-interest that pervades much of contemporary African society, while reaffirming the redemptive quality of laughter and a celebratory attitude toward life.

The idea of change is also central to *Until Further Notice,* and the villagers' incapacity to comprehend the full significance of this change is a primary source of the laughter that the play evokes among African audiences. For example, Abessolo admits he received no bride-price before his daughter's marriage. He acknowledges that times have changed and intimates that the return on their investment in Matalina's education will be received in the form of gifts, jobs for her relatives, and opportunities to visit the city for long periods of time. He even expects to collect the entire salary that Matalina earns as a nurse. At the end of the play, he and the other villagers are satisfied, because they see the doctor's gifts of food and drink as the first installment on a never-ending repayment of the debt he owes them. In reality Matalina and her husband have sent the gifts as a substitute for their own presence in Mvoutessi, and the cold, formal tone of the doctor's letter suggests that he does not accept the communal solidarity on which their claims to a portion of his wealth are based. As in *Three Suitors: One Husband,* the young woman in *Until Further Notice* is regarded by her relatives as a potential source of wealth. What they fail to realize is that the very conditions that make this new wealth possible will ultimately limit their access to it.

Nevertheless, their desire to pursue their own material self-interest is similar to the motivation behind the social climbing that takes place in the city. In *Until Further Notice,* this social climbing is portrayed largely through the secondhand accounts of Matalina's brother Mézoé, who had visited her in Yaoundé. He reports how Matalina shops only in European stores, goes to the movies, delights in giving orders to the nurses' aides under her supervision, and hires others to prepare meals that are served at place settings with seven forks. He also relates how she opposed her husband's dreams of working in a backcountry hospital, because that would have taken her away from the possessions and privileges to which she had become accustomed. Thus, his acceptance of an administrative position in Yaoundé represents the triumph of an individualistic ethic over a sense of communal responsibility that might have contributed to the well-being of the entire country.

Mézoé himself acted according to his own economic self-interest by appropriating his sister's motorbike and bringing it back to Mvoutessi. Like Abessolo and the others, he wants something for himself. In any case, he assumes that Matalina's husband could easily replace the motorbike with a new car. His own calculations resemble those of Africa's newly wealthy elites, who also take whatever they want and insouciantly deny that they are living at the expense of others. When Mézoé declares that Africa must change, he is implying that people should become more like Matalina and her husband. Ironically, the widespread acceptance of the need to act in one's own economic self-interest already represents a change in this direction. Most people do not recognize the corruption and alienation toward which this attitude is leading them.

But they do retain an ability to dance, to sing, to laugh, and to celebrate life—a fact highlighted by the festivities announced by Abessolo at the end of the play. These festivities do not constitute a solution to the deep-lying social problems adumbrated in the play; in fact, Oyônô-Mbia has repeatedly warned critics against interpreting the endings of his dramas as solutions. Yet a definite set of values clearly emerges from a careful reading of *Until Further Notice*. It is the same as that which informs the comic vision behind *Three Suitors: One Husband,* and it resembles in many ways the ethos embedded in the Kulu tales, which emphasize the harshness of a world governed by the interplay of forces, not the demands of justice. In such a world, man's most important virtue is his capacity to penetrate deceptive appearances with his intellect. As a corrective to the earnestness with which people pursue materialistic goals in contemporary African society, Oyônô-Mbia furthermore proposes that the celebration of life can redeem them from their own follies. In the background of all his plays, there is thus the wisdom of a comic genius that draws heavily upon traditional African precedent to transform European-style theater into a hybrid genre capable of reaching mass audiences.

Seydou Badian's approach to theater is quite different. His *Death of Chaka* is a play of ideas rather than a comic entertainment with socially critical overtones. He had already served for nearly a year as Minister of Rural Development and Planning in Mali when he began writing it. Like many young intellectuals in Africa, Badian was a committed socialist who resented the humiliations imposed upon the continent by a history of colonialist oppression. To comprehend such feelings, one has merely to recall the disdain in which Europeans held African civilization until very recently. As late as 1962 (the same year in which *The Death of Chaka* was published for the first time), the well-known British historian Hugh Trevor-Roper publicly proclaimed that there was no history in Africa before the arrival of Europeans—only darkness. In view of such attitudes, Badian's preface takes on a heightened significance, for in referring to the historical Chaka, king of the Zulus in southern Africa and brilliant organizer of a 400,000-man army, he is offering evidence to support his conviction that there was not only history before the arrival of the white man but there were also great heroes who succeeded in forging political order from chaos. On one level, then, the play promotes an African sense of pride in history, for by depicting the Zulu leader as a noble idealist and linking him with the creation of a new nation, Badian is ascribing epic proportions to a story that had been treated in a negative fashion by European historians, who tended to regard the historical Chaka as a bloodthirsty tyrant. Badian's choice of an historical subject thus reflects a desire to recover the truth and to refute ethnocentric commentators like Trevor-Roper.

His specific choice of Chaka was undoubtedly influenced by the fact that the most illustrious francophone African writer of the postwar period, the president of Senegal Léopold Sédar Senghor, had written a long poem on Chaka, transforming him from a cruel despot into a sensitive spokesman for the ideology of negritude. Senghor's attention had been drawn to the figure of Chaka by the Reverend V. Ellenburger's French translation of Thomas Mofolo's Sotho epic about him. As a Christian from a non-Zulu tribe, Mofolo had no interest in glorifying his subject. On the contrary, he portrays Chaka as a powerful, charismatic leader who overcame illegitimacy and exile to become chief of his own small Ngoni tribe and then, through conquest and political acumen, the founder of the Zulu nation. Where there had been a congeries of warring tribes, he imposed political unity and the rule of law. In part, his success was due to his brilliance as a military strategist, for he introduced new ways of fighting and inspired a fierce sense of loyalty among his followers, although several of his generals broke away from his command and established a new nation to the north.

It is difficult to disentangle truth from legend in the story of Chaka's early nineteenth-century reign in southern Africa before the arrival of the Europeans, but the larger outlines of Mofolo's story no doubt conform to historical fact; however, his specific characterization of Chaka is deeply tinged with a Christian interpretation of man's propensity for evil. In Mofolo's version of the story, Chaka's success is purchased at the expense of his soul, for the sorcerer Isanusi, whom he met in the forest during his exile, tempts him to seek power and to repudiate personal ties. Thus, his Chaka not only massacres whole tribes of people, he has his wife and his mother put to death as well. At the end of Mofolo's epic, Chaka has gone completely mad and is fleeing from his own court when his half brothers Dingana and Mhlagana assassinate him.

When Senghor decided to adapt the Chaka legend for his own purposes, he focused upon the Zulu leader's dying moments. Against the accusatory voice of a white European, Senghor's Chaka justifies himself as the man who sacrificed his own personal desires to the liberation and unification of his people. He describes his murders as the burning of fields so that new crops can grow, or as the grinding of wheat to produce flour. The values that characterize Chaka's stance are precisely the negritude values that the Senegalese poet-president had repeatedly proclaimed: the dignity of black people, rhythm, the capacity for joy, a respect for tradition. As he himself has admitted, Senghor projected his own dilemma onto the figure of the dying Chaka, for he sees himself as a man who chose political life at the expense of his poetic inclinations. From this perspective, Chaka becomes the embodiment of everything that Africa has to offer the rest of the world in Senghor's utopian vision of a *métissage* ("cross-breeding," "blending") of cultures.

However, this image of Chaka was not at all what Badian had in mind as a historical model for the postcolonial period in Africa. He obviously agreed with Senghor in regard to the need for a new black dignity, and he too sought to recover a heroic African past that had been completely misunderstood by European historians; however, Badian rejected Senghor's emphasis upon authenticity as well as his romanticizing of the process of liberation. For him the crucial issue was the need to devise a pragmatic approach to the creation of unified, economically viable African nations in the aftermath of colonial exploitation. He was convinced that such a task requires the presence of a charismatic leader who could inspire people from a variety of different ethnic backgrounds to work toward the ideal of a just and equitable society. To accomplish this task, the leader must possess superior organizational skills and a solid grasp of the possibilities for technological innovation.

Under the direction of such a leader, the people will have to display a spirit of self-sacrifice and an unwavering loyalty to his commands if the long-range goal of a self-respecting, prosperous nation is ever to be attained. The greatest threat to the emergence of a viable African nation was, Badian felt, the people's desire to slacken their efforts and to consume what little wealth their country had managed to acquire. In his opinion, the privileged classes, including military officers, would be particularly prone to adopt such a counterproductive attitude. During the early 1960s Kwame Nkrumah,

Introduction

Patrice Lumumba, and Sekou Touré seemed to offer the sort of enlightened socialist leadership that Badian had in his mind, although their methods were already being contested in their own countries and abroad. Lumumba had been killed by the time *The Death of Chaka* was published in 1962. Nkrumah would be toppled in a coup several years later, and Touré evolved into a dictatorial figure.

Nevertheless, Badian had an important point to make, and he chose the historical figure of Chaka to make it, for his Chaka becomes a model for political leadership in contemporary Africa. Chaka's ruthless suppression of entire peoples and his imposition of a harsh discipline upon his followers are the necessary price that must be paid, according to Badian, if a new nation is to arise from postcolonial chaos and become a peaceful, unified community. From this perspective, Badian's Chaka is a savior who sacrifices himself for the future well-being of everyone in his realm. When he is assassinated at the end of the play by three of his generals, he falls victim to the privileged elites and their desire for a life of ease. Thus, in addition to recovering a sense of pride in Africa's heroic past, Badian employs the story of Chaka to illustrate the validity of his own ideological position in a larger African debate over the course to be followed in the development of new nations on the continent.

The Death of Chaka is essentially a dialogue of conflicting perspectives. First, Chaka is presented through the eyes of his rebellious generals. Although there is an undercurrent of recognition for his accomplishments, these men are disturbed by what they interpret as Chaka's arbitrary cruelty and self-aggrandizing tendencies. Beneath the surface of their comments, it becomes apparent that some of them are also jealous of him. And they are all tired of the continuous effort that he demands from them. The specific occasion for their discussion in the opening scenes is Chaka's announcement that the Zulu will attack a coalition of hostile tribes in the south in order to consolidate their previous victories and to remove the last major threat to their control in the area. In addition, the generals resent the fact that Chaka had recently removed them from their command of specific regiments (*impis*) and would henceforth assign them to their positions only shortly before the battle. The immediate objective of the generals is to prevent the battle from taking place, for they regard it as untimely and unreasonable.

As their conversations progress, however, they gradually persuade themselves that it is necessary to eliminate Chaka, whom they accuse of being mad and increasingly bloodthirsty. Their arguments appear credible, and the reader of the play is predisposed to judge Chaka unfavorably. Yet when Chaka himself appears on the stage relatively late in the play, their image of him is utterly discredited, and they themselves are revealed for what they are—petty, self-serving plotters against the legitimate authority of a genuine leader. Badian adopts this approach for a very good reason. Because the truly decisive socialist leaders of independent African nations are frequently maligned by local elites and by conservative interests in the industrialized world, he desires to make the case against such leaders appear plausible so that when it is revealed as fraudulent, the audience will gain insight into the way people are duped in the real world by similar, apparently valid arguments. The drama of Badian's play lies, not in the action, but in this conflict of ideas. His major purpose in drawing upon the story of an early nineteenth-century African hero is to raise the level of consciousness about what needs to be done in the present.

At first the generals' case against Chaka appears strong. They speak with abhorrence about the annihilation of entire tribes, massacres, and the burning of villages. They claim that Chaka has obliged them to carry out senselessly cruel orders, and they accuse him of killing his own followers for trivial and arbitrary reasons. Because they had acquired all the wealth they can use, they see no further purpose in fighting. As Mhlagana suggests, it is time for them to live in peace and to enjoy the fruits of their labors. Under these circumstances, they discuss the various ways they might oppose Chaka. Ini-

tially Dingana and Mapo are in favor of speaking directly to
the Zulu leader and sharing their concerns with him, but they
are eventually persuaded by Mhlagana's argument that merely
talking to a bloodthirsty tyrant will only result in their own
deaths. Thus, Dingana shifts his position from support for a
more moderate approach to advocacy for a plan to betray
Chaka to the enemy on the eve of battle, and Mapo, who
holds out the longest, eventually joins the other two in as-
sassinating Chaka at the end of the play. In short, the generals
succeed in rationalizing their act on the basis of their conviction that Chaka is unfit to rule.

Although their position seems reasonable at first, it is undercut in several ways—by the force of opposing arguments,
by the results of Chaka's actions, and by a growing awareness
of the actual motivations behind their line of reasoning. Mhlagana and Dingana are Chaka's half brothers, and they are obviously jealous of Chaka's fame and his popularity among the
people. Ironically, they themselves would have had nothing if
Chaka's organizational and political genius had not brought
the Zulu nation into being. Mapo himself recalls how the
weak, squabbling tribes in the area had been subject to ma-
rauding animal predators and to the exactions of neighboring
peoples. He reminds the other generals how Chaka had
taught them to fight and how he had given them a new confidence in their own destiny. His reference to a Chaka solicitous
for the welfare of his people clashes with their accusations
against him. Yet even Mapo believes that too much blood has
been shed and that Chaka demands too much of his men. This
judgment ultimately aligns him with Dingana and Mhlagana,
but his hesitancy casts serious doubt upon the objectivity of
their depiction of Chaka as a tyrant. It also demonstrates the
extent to which their personal motivations color their con-
demnation of the Zulu leader.

Furthermore, the generals are indecisive and defeatist. By
the time they have made up their minds to undertake a particular course of action, Chaka has already begun to act, confronting them with a fait accompli and nullifying their plans.

They repeatedly overestimate obstacles and underestimate the commitment of their own troops. They contend that the march to the battlefield will take at least eight days, but Chaka accomplishes it in five; they argue that their men cannot fight without resting for several days, but Chaka leads them into battle on the following morning without the aid of the rebellious generals and achieves his greatest victory against an overwhelmingly superior number of enemy soldiers. The point is that a nation can forge its own greatness if its people internalize a noble ideal, sacrifice present pleasures for the future of their society, and follow the inspired leadership of the individual who translates the ideal into a practical course of action. By the end of the play, the generals are revealed as petty-minded opponents of the true nation-building process—men led astray by their own ambitions, their jealousies, their desire for a life of ease, and their failure to grasp the nature of the ideal for which Chaka is fighting. In light of the frequent coups that have beset Africa during the first three decades of independence, Badian's analysis of the generals' mentality seems almost prophetic.

The generals' case against Chaka is further undercut by the intervention of two individuals who remain steadfastly loyal to him. As a young girl, Notibe had been saved from the jaws of a hyena by the intrepid Chaka. In contrast to the generals, she moves from a willingness to question Chaka's actions to a wholehearted endorsement of the ideal he represents. Ndlebe is a young general who has devoted himself wholeheartedly to the cause. Both of them reinforce the Chaka image implied by Mapo's comments. On the basis of their testimony, Chaka emerges as the liberator of an enslaved and humiliated people. They counter the generals' arguments by pointing out that bloodshed and decisive action are necessary if people hope to escape the predations of wild animals and the designs of those who desire to subjugate them. Neither attaches great importance to personal possessions or present pleasures, because they realize that concerted effort and self-sacrifice are needed to fulfill a great destiny. What Chaka did, they claim, was to restore a people's lost pride in itself. As Ndlebe says, "if we are what we are, it is because we had a leader who knew how to organize us, who knew how to guide us, who knew how to give the whole people that confidence without which there can be no victories." Like Notibe, he sees through the general's false arguments and rededicates himself to the greatness of the Zulu nation that Chaka has brought into being. For this reason, he rebukes the generals for failing to understand that a prerequisite of greatness is the ability to work together in the service of an ideal. "You think obedience lowers you," he lectures them. "You are mistaken. Obedience lowers no one; on the contrary, it makes you great." The statements of Notibe and Ndlebe thus present a counterimage to the one adduced by the generals in defense of their rebellious intentions.

The strongest argument in favor of Chaka's approach to nation-building is Chaka himself. Although he does not make his first appearance until late in the play, the audience knows from the moment he steps on the stage that he is not the despot depicted by the generals. Whereas they are indecisive and preoccupied with their own safety, he is decisive and concerned for the future welfare of the Zulu nation. Whereas they constantly fear the possibility of defeat, he confidently pursues the goal he has set for his people, and he is willing to sacrifice his own personal comfort with that end in mind. Throughout the play, there are allusions to Chaka's special relationship to the supreme god Nkulun-kulu, suggesting that his creation of a new and proud nation represents a divinely ordained mission. He himself tells Notibe the story of his encounter with the Lord of the Deep Water, who had assured him long before he came to power that he bore within himself the greatness of his people, because he preferred their collective greatness to any personal happiness he might be able to attain. This anecdote symbolizes Chaka's commitment and helps explain how he was able to inspire a similar comportment among the younger people of the Zulu nation. Before the battle against the confederation of tribes from the south, both Ndlebe and Notibe express to him their faith in his enterprise, and after the glorious victory, the young men and women salute him as a god-sent messenger. What he represents for them is the ideal of generous, self-sacrificing commitment to the future of an entire people. Both in his actions and in his impact upon these young men and women, Chaka reveals himself as a genuine hero, just the opposite of what the generals had described him as being.

In a superficial sense, the generals prevail. Humiliated by the fact that Chaka had disdained their support in defeating the southern alliance by his clever military strategy, they follow him into the darkness as he walks alone from the camp to commune with Nkulun-kulu. Even then the generals are afraid to face him, for they plunge their knives into his back. He dies, but like Christ, he leaves behind him an idea that will germinate in the minds of others and ultimately will triumph over the legacy of those who killed him. In a more profound sense, therefore, Chaka is victorious over Dingana, Mhlagana, and Mapo. With his dying breath, Chaka mocks them, because he forsees that the impending arrival of the white man will once again bring oppression to the land of the Zulu. Not only will the generals fail to gain any advantage from their betrayal of him, they will be subjected, as he says, to the "long night" of colonial rule. Ironically, it is the spirit of Chaka that will survive this long night. Remaining alive in the memories of the Zulu people, it will someday inspire a new Chaka to arise and lead them once again out of their servitude. That is why he insists that Notibe tell his story to her children. Yet a new Chaka will only succeed if the people are united in their willingness to follow him, and that is the message that Badian wants to leave with contemporary African audiences. In short, his version of Chaka's death serves to outline the ideological stance he regards as necessary for the success of the nation-building process in postcolonial Africa.

In this sense, Chaka becomes the bearer of a divinely sanctioned message to all Africans. Yet in assuming his mission as the creator of a new nation, he suffers the tragedy that so many leaders in contemporary Africa have had to confront.

Despite his idealism and the force of his personality, his commitment to the greatness of his people is susceptible to being interpreted as a desire for self-aggrandizement, and his successes provoke jealousy among the very people who have profited the most from his rise to power. Chaka realizes that the creation of a nation can never be accomplished without work and sacrifice; cruelties will be inflicted on many, and the burden will be heavy to carry. As he himself says, the exercise of power is like a clear pool of water; the sand at the bottom may appear pure, but it is often mixed with mud. In other words, when a leader works for the benefit of an entire society, harsh measures will have to be adopted, and some people will suffer. The water in the pool will become murky. Similarly, when a ruler seeks to reach an idealistic goal, he may well contribute to that suffering. This idea emerges even more clearly when Chaka explains what he has attempted to do for the Zulu: "man is an animal with two heads. One is named Greatness, the other Mediocrity. Greatness is born out of sacrifice and suffering. Mediocrity grows on idleness, indifference, and pleasure. I wanted to cut this head from my people, but it is difficult to overcome it. It is like the mushrooms that spring up after the rain." The process of rooting out indolence and self-indulgence is necessarily a painful one, as Chaka's beheading image suggests. But the pain must be endured if the goal is to be reached.

To sustain the effort needed to create a new nation, Chaka must expend an enormous amount of energy, and even before his final battle he feels "strangely weary." Isanusi explains to him that he has fulfilled his destiny by transforming a chaotic, undisciplined group of warring tribes into a unified and self-respecting nation. "A new people has been born," he declares. "It was to achieve this that Nkulun-kulu, the Almighty, sent you. Your work has been accomplished, and so, too, has your destiny." Isanusi thus reaffirms the idea that Chaka is a god-sent hero whose actions convey a crucial message to his people—a message that will be the key to their liberation in the future, after the long night of colonial oppression will have passed. On a personal level, however, he must pay a heavy price for serving as the instrument of destiny. Once again like Christ, he must sacrifice his own life so that his message can take root in the minds of others. Chaka does suffer a tragic fate on the personal level, but his story is actually an optimistic tragedy on the social level, because it holds out the promise of dignity, independence, and future greatness for his people.

According to Badian, the newly independent states of Africa have it within their power to realize this promise, if they adopt the attitudes he depicts favorably in *The Death of Chaka*. First, the people must believe in themselves and in their historic destiny as a free and independent national community. Second, a charismatic leader needs to emerge, for he alone can inspire the people to pursue the ideal of a just and equitable future society; he is also the one who can marshal them into a disciplined social order capable of exploiting the natural world for their mutual benefit, while reconciling internal differences and commanding respect from the rest of the world. Third, the people must recognize their national leader and follow him in the knowledge that their collective purpose can only be achieved through heroic effort and self-sacrifice; the greatest danger to the modern African state is, Badian implies, the tendency of the new elites to prefer personal wealth and comfort over the common welfare, for their perquisites are bought at the expense of foreign domination.

In the play, Chaka himself summarizes this ideological position when he exhorts his youthful followers always to remember why they had won their greatest victory. We were victorious, he tells them, "because we knew how to obey, because we knew what we wanted, because we were able to forget ourselves for the sake of a unity we believed greater than the individual." This speech contains the essence of Badian's political philosophy; in fact, it might well serve as a prescription for the qualities he regards as paramount in the nation-building process—obedience to a central authority, a sense of common purpose, and a willingness to sacrifice one's own personal goals for the benefit of others, particularly those of future generations.

In looking back over the history of African independence since the publication of Badian's play in 1962, one can see the value of his advice. The elites in many countries have rebelled against legitimate authority, and their relative comfort has often been purchased at the price of continuing foreign domination. A lack of clarity in regard to national objectives and a failure to reconcile internal conflicts has brought many African nations to the brink of socioeconomic chaos. Nevertheless, a fundamental question about the possibility of tyranny remains unanswered in Badian's play. The massacres of dissident tribes, the burning of peaceful villages, and the execution of one's own soldiers cannot in themselves bring about a harmonious and productive community. On the contrary, they often breed resentment and fear among the survivors.

Badian implies that the leader of a new nation has to take upon himself the burden of guilt arising from such actions. He is suggesting that the ends justify the means. However, the recent history of Africa demonstrates the abuses to which such an attitude can lead. Millions of Africans have died as the result of policies implemented by dictators in the name of national unity. Although readers can be moved to admire the skill with which Badian draws upon history to propound a political ideology for twentiety-century Africa, they cannot help but reflect on the more difficult questions he leaves unanswered. To what extent do idealistic, nation-building goals justify the adoption of cruel, coercive practices? Can a particular leader's mission of national unity cost too much in terms of human suffering? And how can the successful military organization of Chaka be redirected toward the more difficult task of creating a harmonious socioeconomic structure in poverty-stricken African countries? In retrospect, such questions seem central to any discussion of nation-building in Africa, but during the early 1960s, the young Malian Minister of Rural Development and Planning was preoccupied with the need to move quickly toward a new sense of national unity,

Introduction

and his blueprint for development has the merit of defining the choices that face all recently independent countries.

The plays of Oyônô-Mbia and Badian are strikingly different. *Three Suitors: One Husband* and *Until Further Notice* are social comedies that draw upon village life for their subject matter and reveal an underlying skepticism about the possibility of human progress. *The Death of Chaka* is a historical tragedy that conveys a heroically optimistic attitude toward the creation of new African nations. The plays of Oyônô-Mbia are entertainments that must be seen upon the stage to be fully appreciated. Badian's drama contains a serious statement of ideological commitment, and the complexity of its argument can best be understood by reading it. Nevertheless, placing them together in a single volume is instructive, for it illustrates the breadth of theatrical activity that has taken place in francophone Africa since the earliest days of national independence.

Richard Bjornson
The Ohio State University

Three Suitors:
One Husband

For Pierre and Gisèle Fichet, and for all our friends at the Collège Evangélique de Libamba, with love . . .

Author's Note

The play is set in Mvoutessi, in the southern part of East Cameroun. A typical Bulu village, built along the road. The actors will normally be sitting in front of Atangana's main house. The kitchen, a separate building, is seen at the far end of the stage. A hedge separates the village from the road, which latter might be suggested by the noise of cars coming and going at long intervals. Seats include old local lawn chairs made of bush ropes or antelope skins, old wooden stools, etc.

Juliette, a daughter of the village, is about to return home from her secondary school with Oko, her fiancé, whom she intends to introduce to her family. But other arrangements for her future had already been made by her father, Atangana, and all her relatives expect her to comply with these. The resulting clash symbolises the meeting of two conflicting cultures.

Throughout the comedy, the audience will learn something about the major problem facing Africans today: is it possible to make room for the new while at the same time preserving the old? The Viper episode in Act Three may be taken as an illustration of this. Certain animals like vipers, wild boars, etc., were 'taboo' to women: the younger men weren't expected to eat them until they had been granted special permission to do so by the elders of the tribe.

THREE SUITORS: ONE HUSBAND was written in French in 1960 and first publicly staged in Yaoundé, Cameroun in 1961. It was translated into English by the author and given its first performance in Britain at the University of Keele in February 1967, by the Keele Drama Group with the following cast:

ATANGANA	Ray Johnson
ABESSOLO, his father	Ami Yeshurun
ONDUA, his brother	Rick Burningham
BELLA, his mother	Bobbie Conn
MATALINA, Ondua's daughter	Shariffa Jamal
OYONO, Atangana's son	John Munday
MAKRITA, Atangana's wife	Jane Parkin
JULIETTE, Atangana's daughter	Jan Allen
MBARGA, the village headman	Mike Perkins
MEZOE, a relative	Ian Pitcairn
KOUMA, Juliette's cousin	Dave Whitebread
OKO, her fiance	Bernard Dutton
NDI, the first suitor	Ian Jones
MBIA, the second suitor	John Griffin
TCHETGEN, the third suitor	Ian Jones
SANGA-TITI, the witch-doctor	Tim Fletcher
ENGULU, Mbia's driver	Tony Lambe
WITCH-DOCTOR'S ASSISTANT	Pamela Groves
MUSICIANS	

Produced by Guillaume Oyônô-Mbia
Costumes and sets by Rose Chue

ACT ONE

A quiet afternoon in Mvoutessi. When the curtain rises, the actors present at the beginning of the act are seen in front of ATANGANA's main house. ATANGANA is making a basket. He now and then casts an impatient glance at a huge alarm-clock set before him. ABESSOLO is busy sculpting an ebony figurine, smoking a long pipe, and chasing flies with a fly-whisk. ONDUA and OYONO are playing a game of 'songho', and making frequent use of a calabash of palm-wine set beside them. OYONO will be going now and then to pour some wine for his father and grandfather. The women do not drink, of course. Instead, MATALINA has a basketful of peanuts set beside her, which she is cracking. BELLA will join and help her when she enters. All this should be done normally throughout the act. Mvoutessi is, after all, a quiet little village in the bush where events like those we are about to recount do not occur every day.

ATANGANA (scandalised, pointing at the clock): You see, Ondua? The clock itself says we're half-way through the afternoon already!

(Glancing towards the road.)

And that wife of mine's still working in the bush! Will that woman ever understand that she must always come back to the village well before midday?

ONDUA (with a gesture of discouragement): Ah, ka, Atangana! Don't talk about that! It's only what I always say: women will have their way! No sensible man should waste his time trying to reason with them! . . . Take my wife Monica, for instance: only yesterday, I was asking her to give me one bottle, just one bottle of that brandy . . .

(He speaks softly, as distilling that local brandy is illegal.)

er . . . 'Arki' . . . which she's distilling . . .

(Louder.)

Only one bottle I asked her to give me! And you know what she did?

MATALINA (she likes teasing her father): She said no, didn't she?

ONDUA (offended by this light treatment of a serious matter): Your mother did worse than that, Matalina! She would only give me one bottle . . . yes, just one bottle!

(Vindictively, while the other men are shaking their heads in sympathy.)

To think that I once . . .

ABESSOLO (with an unmistakable 'didn't I warn you' expression on his face): Ha ha! . . . So you're getting angry, Ondua? Haven't I always said that the men of your generation all behave like foolish people?

(Proudly.)

In my day, when I was still Abessôlô, and . . .

(Pointing at BELLA who is coming from the kitchen.)

my wife was still a woman, do you think I'd have stood for such nonsense? But today, you let your wives wear clothes! You let them eat all sorts of taboo animals! You even ask them their opinion on this and that! . . .

(He pauses to catch his breath.)

Well, what else could you expect?

(Firmly.)

I tell you again, you must beat your wives! Yes, beat them!

(Shaking his fly-whisk at MATALINA.)

And treat your daughters just the same way!

BELLA (now sitting near MATALINA): What's left in this world of today, my poor husband? I see women eating even vipers, wild boars, and . . .

(Clapping her hands in disgust.)

Aa keeaah, Oyônô Eto Mekong ya Ngozip aah!

ATANGANA (hesitantly): My father speaks the truth, but . . .

ABESSOLO: Always a 'but'! Why can't you understand that I always give you good advice? If it hadn't been for me the other day, you wouldn't have taken the money which was paid here by Ndi, the young man from Awae who wants to marry my granddaughter! You said it would've been a better idea to wait and consult Juliette herself before accepting the bride-price!

(Shocked, to the audience.)

Consult a *woman* about her marriage!

MATALINA: And that young man paid one hundred thousand francs at once, like a real suitor!

ATANGANA (he can't help beaming, and proudly beating his chest): Er . . . I must admit, Juliette is the right daughter for a wise man like me! When I sent her to secondary school, I was justly saying to everybody: 'Some day, I'll benefit from that!'

ONDUA: Ah Matalina, Juliette herself is coming back from Dibamba today, isn't she?

MATALINA: Yes, she is! She wrote to me that she'd be here this very afternoon!

ATANGANA: What a happy coincidence! You know, Ndi, the young farmer who paid one hundred thousand francs for her is coming this afternoon as well! Also . . .

(A pause.)

Act One

... er ... I'm told that another suitor, a *great* civil servant from
Sangmélima, is coming to see me today! ...

(Excitedly.)

Coming to see *me*, you hear?

(Confidentially.)

Other people have to wait a long time before they can even *speak* to that
man in the city!

(Excited chatter around.)

BELLA (proudly): A *real* white man! My granddaughter's going to marry a
real white man! Ah ... Nane Ngōk!

MATALINA (who wouldn't really mind being Juliette now): How lucky!
My cousin was definitely born with a star on her forehead! Fancy
marrying a wealthy man! She'll soon have lots of dresses, blonde wigs,
she'll soon have everything!

ONDUA: Ah Atangana, my brother! There's your chance to obtain a gun
permit without the usual fuss!

ABESSOLO (quickly): Yes! Don't miss such an opportunity! Remember
how long you always have to wait in front of Government offices just
because nobody knows you? Now, with such an important son-in-law,
I bet they'll all be going out of their way to attend to you in Sangmélima!

ONDUA: They will! ... they will! ...

(Softly, after cautiously looking around.)

You also know that Medola, police commissioner of Zoetele, keeps
arresting me for being drunk and disorderly, and my wife Monica for
illegally distilling 'Arki'. If we give Juliette to that important civil
servant, we would no longer have anything to fear from the police: as
soon as everybody knows that ...

ATANGANA: You both speak the truth, but you seem to forget the main
thing: how much money is the civil servant going to bring us? Suppose
it's less than Ndi's one hundred thousand francs, how am I going to pay
back the previous bride-price? And how much money will be left in my
pocket?

BELLA: Ah ka, my son! He'll bring a lot of money, I tell you! In my day ...

MATALINA (perhaps speaking from experience): No real civil servant would
go courting without a large sum of money in his pocket!

ONDUA (who never forgets important matters): Above all, I hope he's
bringing us something strong to drink!

OYONO: Who would go visiting people without bringing them something
strong to drink?

MATALINA (as a car is heard stopping): This must be Juliette!

(She runs to the road and disappears, saying.)

It's her!

ATANGANA (with a happy smile): A remarkable coincidence!

OYONO (going towards the road): I'll go and get her suitcase.

ONDUA (to OYONO): Ah Oyôn! Don't tell Juliette about the civil servant yet. Your father will . . .

ATANGANA: Yes! . . . I'll break the good news to her myself! Just go and get her suitcase . . .

(OYONO disappears, but only for a brief moment, as JULIETTE and MATALINA were already coming. JULIETTE embraces OYONO, then leaves her suitcase to him so as to run and embrace all the others in the traditional Bulu way. There will be some confusion; everybody will be expected to make appropriate remarks to the newcomer. BELLA speaks when greeting is over.)

BELLA: You came earlier than usual today, Juliette!

JULIETTE: We came by coach instead of waiting for the train.

OYONO (now taking the suitcase to the main house): I thought you had!

MATALINA: How are your studies, Juliette?

JULIETTE (not too modestly): Well . . . I passed, that's the main thing!

BELLA (jumping up as excitedly as she can): She passed again! My granddaughter passed again! Ah Nane Ngôk!

(She utters the women's traditional cry of joy, the 'oyenga'.)

Ou-ou-ou . . .

ABESSOLO (with a pleased smile): You . . . you're still studying at Dibamba, aren't you, my child?

JULIETTE (bursts out laughing): At Li . . . Libamba, come on, Tita! Haven't I explained the difference to you again and . . .

ATANGANA (laughing too): Your grandfather's getting old, Juliette! . . . But tell me, how are your white teachers, the French, the Americans, and the missionaries?

JULIETTE: They're all right, father! We're expecting to have even more teachers next year!

MATALINA (foolishly, while the men are making frantic gestures at her to shut up): Next year? Is your husband going to let you go back to school? Or will he . . .

(ONDUA has stopped her by tapping her gently on the shoulder, but it is too late: JULIETTE is now staring at the others.)

JULIETTE: My husband? Which husband? Have I got a husband?

BELLA (she too is unaware of the men's uneasiness): A husband, did you

say? Why, you've already got two of them, Juliette! To think that some
girls . . .

ATANGANA (resentfully): Aa keeaa, come on, both of you! You know very
well that I promised to break the good news to her myself!

(He scratches his head in search of the best way to start.)

I'll tell you all about it, my child! A young man came to see us five
weeks ago, and said he wanted to marry you. Of course, because of
your education and value we decided to take the one hundred thousand
francs he paid . . .

(JULIETTE is startled, and he adds quickly.)

but to lay that money aside! . . . You see, we're expecting a great civil
servant here this afternoon!

(Leaning forward, for JULIETTE to realise how very lucky she is.)

He too wants to marry you!

(A pause.)

Of course, if he pays me a larger bride-price . . .

JULIETTE (indignantly): What? Am I for sale? Are you trying to give me
to the highest bidder? Why can't you ask me my opinion about my own
marriage?

(All the others remain speechless with surprise. While JULIETTE was
speaking, ATANGANA's proud smile had gradually turned into a shocked
grin: this was certainly not the grateful reaction he was expecting.)

ABESSOLO (standing up, to JULIETTE): Your opinion?

(To the audience.)

She wants to be asked her opinion!

(To JULIETTE.)

Since when do women speak in Mvoutessi? Who teaches you girls of
today such disgraceful behaviour? Why are you always trying to have a
say in every matter? Aren't you happy that your whole family made such
a wise decision in your favour?

JULIETTE (pleading): But I haven't even seen the man you want me to
marry! How can you expect me to love him?

(At hearing this nonsense, ABESSOLO stares at the others, most of
whom are now shaking their hands in disbelief: they never knew
JULIETTE could be so stupid.)

MATALINA: But he's a very important man, Juliette: a civil servant!

JULIETTE (stubbornly): I . . .

BELLA: Matalina's right! Any sensible girl would be proud of such an
opportunity! Now, in my day . . .

Three Suitors: One Husband

ABESSOLO (to the audience): Did you hear that? She wants to see the great man before agreeing to love him!

(To JULIETTE again.)

Isn't that civil servant going to give us all lots of money to marry you? What more could any man do to deserve a girl's love?

(Suspiciously.)

Or perhaps you too are trying to act like so many disobedient girls of today who run off to marry young men as poor as flies, no money, no offices, no cars, no nice clothes, these girls who leave their families as poor as before?

JULIETTE (angrily): So you were expecting me to make you rich! Am I a shop, or some other source of income?

(There are exclamations of shocked surprise around. OYONO comes back to the stage, having left his sister's suitcase in the main house. He is bringing her a chair but she refuses to take it, and sulkily sits on the floor. OYONO is puzzled for a moment, then he joins ONDUA who gives him a soft and brief summary of the situation while MATALINA is speaking to JULIETTE.)

MATALINA (incredulously): How can you say that, Juliette? Do you really expect to be happy with a penniless husband? What would he give your family?

ONDUA (proudly): You're a good daughter to me and your mother Monica, Matalina! These words show that you'll try and make us rich when you get married!

ABESSOLO (triumphantly): That proves what I always say: never send your daughters to secondary school! Look at Matalina who never went to secondary school! Doesn't she always speak like a sensible and obedient girl?

(Shaking his fly-whisk at JULIETTE.)

But if you don't watch out, Juliette's certainly going to marry some unimportant man who won't even be able to find one hundred thousand francs to give us as a down payment for the marriage! Yea a ah! This world is no longer what it used to be! Schools have corrupted everything!

(He sits down like an overwhelmed man.)

Everything!

BELLA (approvingly): Aa ahmm! In my day . . .

(MAKRITA comes back from the bush, with a basket containing food — cassava, banana, sugar cane, etc. — on her back. As soon as JULIETTE sees her, she goes to embrace her. ATANGANA speaks some time later.)

ATANGANA (pointing at the clock again): You see how late my wife's coming back from the bush? The clock itself says . . .

Act One

MAKRITA: I went down to have a look at my corn field, near the river Sô ô.

BELLA: Have the monkeys caused any more damage since we last went there?

MAKRITA: I think they'll simply ruin the crop this season, Na' Bella! It's dreadful!

ONDUA (approving): Dreadful! Monica said to me the other day that we might never get enough corn to . . .

(Softly and cautiously as usual.)

distill any more 'Arki' . . .

(To OYONO who is now taking a bunch of bananas out of his mother's basket.)

Ah Oyôn! I think it's high time you went and laid a few monkey traps around your mother's field.

OYONO (walking back to his seat): I'm waiting for Ndi: he's very good at laying monkey traps . . .

MAKRITA (happy to hear that): Is he? So much the better!

(To JULIETTE.)

Your father's giving you a very hard-working husband, my daughter! You should have seen him and your brother Oyônô clearing the patch of land where I'm growing peanuts this season!

BELLA: Very hard-working . . .

ABESSOLO (impatiently): Yes, but we don't want him any more! We want Juliette to marry the civil servant!

MAKRITA (with a surprised look at JULIETTE): The civil servant?

ONDUA (beaming): Yes! A great civil servant who's bringing us many strong drinks from Sangmélima . . .

ATANGANA: And lots of money . . .

(Threateningly, to JULIEFTE.)

And don't you dare to say again that you want to see him before you agree to love him.

JULIETTE: But how can you expect me to . . .

BELLA (scandalised): Juliette! A girl should never speak when her father's speaking!

MAKRITA (in an attempt to divert the conversation): Ah Oyôn! Go and get me a log which I left near the well, in your father's plantation!

(OYONO goes out through the road.)

ONDUA: Ah Makrita! Oyônô should by now be staying with the sages of this village so as to hear what they've got to say!

ATANGANA (shaking a threatening fist at MAKRITA who was going to the kitchen): She's the one who teaches my children such disgraceful behaviour! Just look at Juliette!

MAKRITA (frightened, from the doorstep): Juliette! Haven't I always told you to be obedient to your family? Why don't you try and behave like your cousin Matalina?

JULIETTE: You want me to let them sell me like a goat? After all, I'm a valuable human being!

MATALINA (surprised by such lack of intelligence): Of course you're a valuable human being, Juliette! Haven't you heard that Ndi, the young farmer who came here, paid as much as one hundred thousand francs to marry you? We're also expecting a civil servant who will certainly pay much more money for you. Doesn't all this prove to you that you're a valuable human being as you say?

BELLA (a discouraged sigh): I simply can't understand these girls of today! In my day, only those girls for whom the largest bride-price had been paid were respected. Look here, Juliette do you want to be a disgrace to us all like your cousin Myriam who married a good-for-nothing beggar? A young man who couldn't even give us enough money to . . .

ANTANGANA (who had been following his own thoughts): That civil servant could even help me to obtain a gun permit. You all know how difficult that sort of thing is when one doesn't know the right people in Government offices . . .

JULIETTE (still trying to plead): And you really expect to get all these things through me?

ABESSOLO: Who else do you want us to turn to? You're the most educated daughter we have, and your brother Oyônô must pay for the girl he wants to marry in Ebolowa!

(He pauses: he knows he is going to make a good point.)

Besides, have you already paid us back all the money we spent for your studies at Dibamba and other places?

JULIETTE (slowly, in mounting anger): So you expect me to pay you back?

ABESSOLO (choked with anger, to the audience): Did you hear that? What a stupid girl! A very important civil servant like the one we're expecting this afternoon will make this whole village jealous of your family!

ONDUA: Yes, jealous! Just look at Meka, who once was the poorest man in Messam! He's now so proud ever since his daughter became the twelfth wife of the deputy . . .

ATANGANA (quickly): Of the Secretary of State! A girl who never went to secondary school like Juliette, and who's already had a concrete house

Act One

built for her father!

ABESSOLO (more indignant then ever): And when I think of all that . . .

(He is interrupted by OYONO excitedly running in.)

OYONO: Ah Tita! . . . Tita! . . . The great man! . . . He's here already!

(Confusion among the actors: excited chatter, exclamations, etc. MAKRITA herself comes hurriedly from the kitchen to see what is happening.)

ATANGANA (almost stammering): Er . . . what does he look like?

OYONO (dancing to and fro with excitement): A real civil servant!

ATANGANA (same as above): Er . . . nice clothes?

OYONO (same as above): I tell you again, a real civil servant: he's wearing a superb terylene suit!

BELLA (proudly): A real white man! He's wearing a tyrolean suit!

ABESSOLO (to OYONO): Does he look important?

OYONO (with an eloquent gesture): Important!

ABESSOLO (threateningly, to JULIETTE): And you said you wouldn't love him!

ONDUA (matter-of-factly): Quiet . . . quiet! Ah Oyôn! Did the civil servant bring us something strong to drink?

OYONO: Perhaps he's got wine in his car . . .

MATALINA (excitedly): A car! How lucky, Juliette! You'll no longer have to walk!

MAKRITA (with due maternal pride): Juliette! This is definitely the right husband for a girl like you!

ATANGANA (as practical as usual): If he brings enough money . . .

ONDUA: And enough drinks . . .

ATANGANA: We'll see about all that. Ah Oyôn! Go and beat the drum! Tell everybody in this village to my house this afternoon. Now, let's all go to the road, and meet the great man.

(All the MEN go to the road while all the WOMEN, except JULIETTE, go to the kitchen. JULIETTE looks as dejected as might well be expected and BELLA, who was already on her way to the kitchen, looks back and sees her still sitting on the floor. She therefore walks a few steps back and speaks to JULIETTE, because she thinks there is no need for her to be unduly modest about the happy events.)

BELLA (with a twinkle in her eyes): I always knew my granddaughter would only marry a real white man!

(A drum call is heard as the curtain falls.)

ACT TWO

The same afternoon in Mvoutessi. MBIA is sitting rather conspicuously in a
big armchair which has been set in the middle of the stage. He looks very
important indeed in his fashionable terylene suit. He is also wearing dark
glasses, and an impressive collection of medals on his chest. The servant
ENGULU will now and then pass cigarettes around the grateful villagers,
who will normally help themselves to more than one cigarette at a time.
ENGULU is dressed in a driver's white uniform, complete with oil stains;
in spite of being only the great man's servant, he too looks down on these
bush people because he is, after all, a man from the city. Needless to say, no
woman has been allowed to attend the top-level palaver.

ATANGANA (struggling into his best jacket, which he is putting on because
of the great visitor): O my fathers and brothers of Mvoutessi! I can easily
see that you're asking yourselves: 'Why did Atangana beat the drum to
invite us to his house this afternoon?' Well, I wanted this whole village
to give a big welcome to Mbia, the great civil servant you see here among
us.

(ATANGANA sits down, everybody is now looking at MBIA.)

ABESSOLO: Let the visitor tell us who he is then!

MBIA (after clearing his throat for some time): My name is Mbia. I am a
very important civil servant from Sangmélima. I work in a very large
office.

ALL (extremely impressed): Aaa keeaah!

MBIA (who enjoys the effect): I've been working with the Government for
the last twenty-five years, and the Secretary of State himself knows me
personally.

ALL (same as above): The Secretary of State!

MBIA (exhibiting his chest): Because of my exceptional abilities, I've been
awarded many medals, many distinctions.

ABESSOLO (giving and taking a closer look at MBIA): Here's a real suitor
at last! He's got medals!

MBIA (flattered): Yes . . . great medals! However, so that you may know
me better, I suggest that we have a couple of drinks together . . .

ALL (delightedly looking at one another: this is the moment they had been
waiting for): Aa a ah! There's a real civil servant!

MBARGA (crosses the stage quickly so as to attract MBIA's attention.
Then speaks softly to ATANGANA): Have you already told the civil
servant that I am the headman of this village?

ATANGANA (softly to MBARGA): Not yet, but I'll soon . . .

Act Two

MBARGA (offended, comes forward to speak to the audience): Not yet! Did you hear that? A great man comes here, and he still hasn't thought of introducing to him the greatest man of Mvoutessi!

(Confidentially.)

Just you wait a minute, and you'll see how glad the civil servant will be to meet me!

(Louder to MBIA.)

Mr Civil Servant, my name is Mbarga!

MBIA (absent-mindedly): Mbarga? Hmm, very good . . .

MBARGA: I am the headman of this village!

MBIA (who couldn't care less): The headman? Not bad . . . not bad . . .

MBARGA (to the audience): You see?

(Louder, to MBIA.)

I am the ruler of this whole village!

MBIA (positively annoyed now): All right then! Now, let's have something to drink! Engulu!

ENGULU (rushing forward): Sah?

MBIA: Go and get it!

(ENGULU rushes to the road to get the drinks.)

MBARGA (triumphantly to the audience): What did I tell you? Would the civil servant have given us anything to drink if *I* didn't introduce myself?

ONDUA (softly, to MBARGA): You're the one who will always save us in this village, Ah Mbarga!

MBIA (as ENGULU is bringing a case of beer): Let's start with this!

(ENGULU begins opening bottles and handing them to the villagers who start drinking without bothering about glasses. ONDUA and OYONO help open and hand round the bottles.)

ABESSOLO (as soon as everybody is contentedly drinking): Now, my son, may we know what brings you here?

MBIA (stands up majestically and speaks solemnly): A very important civil servant like me wouldn't be travelling without official reason. Is there anyone among you here who doesn't know the merit of this famous family? Who among you doesn't know that this has always been a family of great people like . . . er . . . er . . .

(He points at ABESSOLO while tapping his own forehead.)

ALL (helpfully): Abessôlô!

MBIA: Yes, Abessôlô! Am I mistaken?

ALL (with expressive gestures of negation): No . . . Te keeaah!

(ABESSOLO is now beaming with pride.)

MBIA: Aren't the villagers of Mvoutessi known everywhere?

ALL (glad to hear a great man acknowledging this): Eeeaah!

MBIA (after a pause): That's why I'm seeking to become a member of this great family through marriage. I ask you to give me Juliette, Atangana's daughter.

(Approving whisper. MBIA sits down.)

ABESSOLO (standing up, to MBIA): You've spoken well, my son. However . . .

(With a questioning glance to the others.)

er . . . before answering your request, we must ask you to tell us your genealogy.

(Some disapproving grunts are heard, but everybody quiets down when MBIA begins speaking.)

MBIA (after a puff from his pipe): I myself belong to the tribe Esse. On my mother's side, I am a descendant of the Mbidambanés. My mother's mother was a Yembông, and the mother of . . .

(There is a general wail of distress when the tribe Yembông is mentioned. MBIA stops in surprise, and looks questioningly at ABESSOLO who is more upset than any of the others.)

ABESSOLO: Yeeeaah! What a pity, my son! the grandmother of Juliette's grandfather was also a Yembông! Impossible marriage.

MBIA (stunned): What?

ABESSOLO (firmly): Impossible marriage!

ALL (angrily): Ah ka, Abessôlô!

ATANGANA (really disappointed): Yeeaah keeaah!

MBIA (furious, getting up): Impossible marriage? And what about my beer?

ABESSOLO (to the others): No marriage . . . no marriage! Return him his beer! He's related to Juliette! No marriage!

MBIA (sharply, to his servant): Engulu! Take back the beer! We're leaving!

ALL (rushing to the case, and helping themselves with more bottles while ENGULU is unsuccessfully trying to take them away): Never. Te keeaah! . . . Te keeaah! . . .

ABESSOLO: Return him his beer . . . Ah ka ka ka!

(He endeavours to take the bottles away from them, but to no avail.)

MBARGA (who has remained unmoved): Kiaah! Kiaah! You'd better reconsider your decision! The civil servant deserves better treatment!

ABESSOLO (horrified): What? Don't you hear he's related to Juliette?

MEZOE (coming closer to ABESSOLO): Ah Abessôlô! Why are you keeping

Act Two

us from drinking what our son-in-law has given us? You'll always be the same in this village: you're trying to cut us out of your family already!

ALL: That's right! He's trying to cut us out!

ONDUA (who is holding at least half a dozen bottles under his arm): O my brother Atangana! Would you really like to see all these middle-aged, respectable men of Mvoutessi leaving our house in dissatisfaction?

ATANGANA (rather undecidedly): No . . . er . . .

ONDUA (with a timid glance towards MBIA): And don't forget that if we reject this important man, it will no longer be safe for us to go to Sangmélima.

(To the others who have been listening.)

Haven't I spoken the truth?

ALL (unanimously): Ea a ah!

MEZOE: Are we going to drink like dumb people?

(He puts down his own bottles in a safe corner.)

Ah Oyônô! Go and get your father's drums!

(OYONO goes to get the drums while MEZOE begins singing.)

Tole m'elae, tole m'elae meyok,
Tole m'elae, Mone Mbidambané,
Tole m'elae . . etc.

(The others join in the chorus, while MEZOE himself sings the solo part. OYONO comes back with two drums. He and ONDUA begin playing the rhythm for the dance 'Nyeng', and MEZOE dances for some time.)

ONDUA (after MEZOE has come to stop the drummers): Quiet . . . quiet . . . Wula wula wula a ah!

ALL (pausing for a while): A a a ah!

ONDUA (singing and dancing as above; MEZOE joins OYONO at the drums, and they play the rhythm of the dance 'Anyeng'):

Aya ya mone minga a a ah,
O lig Ondua a nya'a ve e e . . . ?
aya ya mone minga a a . . . etc.

MBARGA: Wula wula wula a a ah!

ALL: A a a ah!

(They stop altogether.)

MBARGA (his great moment has now come): Listen to me, all of you! I'm the headman of this village! Mbia, our visitor, has come all the way from Sangmélima because he wants to marry our daughter Juliette.

(Casually.)

Well . . . I know that some people here think he's related to Juliette, so there should be no marriage.

(With authority.)

But what? Shall we be foolish enough to turn down a civil servant like Mbia for such reasons? Don't great men always deserve special treatment?

ALL: They do!

MBARGA (winking at MBIA, so as to seek his approbation): Who will make us all very welcome whenever we go to the city?

(MBIA nods.)

ALL: He will!

MBARGA (same as above): Who will always take us to the 'Relais' of Sangmélima, and entertain us like white men there?

ALL: He will!

(ONDUA is seen exulting.)

MBARGA (same as above): Who will set us free from the police?

ALL: Yeeaah! Only him!

(ONDUA waves approvingly at MBARGA who ignores him because he has more important business to attend to.)

MBARGA (almost confidentially): Who knows? Won't Mbia make it possible for us to obtain gun permits and medals of honour?

ALL (noisily): Guns ... guns ... medals ... medals!

MBARGA: Won't he introduce us in all the offices of Sangmélima, even in the Prefect's own office, without delay?

ALL: Without delay!

MBIA (casually): Engulu! One bottle of wine for the headman!

(ENGULU rushes to the road to get the wine.)

MBARGA (encouraged by this start): Our ancestors used to say: 'Important rivers can only be recognised by the size of their tributaries'. I'll therefore ask you: if Mbia is offering us so much to drink now, won't he always be doing so?

ALL (in loud approbation): Eeaaah!

(ENGULU brings a bottle of wine to MBARGA.)

MBARGA (after rubbing the bottle for quite a while): Won't Mbia have the price of our cocoa raised?

ALL: He certainly will!

MBARGA (after a pause): You surprise me very much! When there are important matters to be discussed in this village, you begin talking like a crowd of women, instead of just listening to me!

(Moving towards his seat.)

Act Two

I won't say anything more: carry on by yourselves!

ALL (pleadingly): Speak . . . speak . . . Don't sit down, Mbarga!

MBARGA (sulkily): Never again!

ABESSOLO (moving closer to MBARGA): Ah Mbarga! If you refuse to speak who else will? Ah Oyôn! Go and catch me a chicken for the headman!

(OYONO runs to the kitchen.)

MBARGA (quickly getting up): I'll speak then!

(He resumes his previous stand in the front of the stage.)

Is there anyone in this village who doesn't know that I am a very wise man?

ALL: We all know!

MBARGA: Ah Abessôlô!

ABESSOLO (who was returning to his seat): Here I am!

MBARGA: Didn't I see all our dead fathers once in a dream? Didn't all our dead fathers bless me?

ABESSOLO (very sincerely): They did!

MBARGA: Didn't you see that, my dream?

ABESSOLO (same as above): With my own eyes! I saw your dream! I did!

(A pause during which OYONO brings the chicken to MBARGA.)

MBARGA (to the other villagers): And you were going to reject such an important suitor! A man who's so popular in Sangmélima! A man I've often seen with the Secretary of State himself . . .

MBIA (flattered): Engulu! Two bottles of wine for the headman!

MBARGA (quickly, as ENGULU is running to the road): Who will soon be elected Mayor . . .

MBIA (shouting): Engulu! Four bottles!

(ENGULU returns to the road before being able to bring the previous two bottles.)

MBARGA (same as above): Deputy . . .

MBIA: Engulu! Ten bottles!

(One can hear the noise of many bottles being awkwardly handled on the road.)

MBARGA (striking the floor with his stick): Secretary of State! . . .

MBIA (jumping up in excitement: this has always been his pet dream): Engulu! A whole case of wine!

(He goes to shake hands with MBARGA. However, ENGULU, who was already on his way back with ten bottles of wine, tries to turn sharply so

Three Suitors: One Husband

as to go and get the whole case. Unfortunately, he gets entangled in his bagging pants, and falls just between the two great men who were about to shake hands. MBARGA therefore thinks it more appropriate to help pick up the bottles of wine. ONDUA will give him a hand, of course.)

ABESSOLO (giving up, when the exictement has abated): Forgive me, my son!

(He takes MBIA to his armchair again.)

I didn't realise you were such an important man! You see, I'm only a poor old man . . . but never mind, never mind! We'll forget about your being related to our daughter Juliette!

MBIA (sitting down): Engulu! Four bottles of wine for the grandfather!

(ENGULU runs to the road as usual.)

ABESSOLO: However, there's just one condition: how did you come?

(All listen intently: this must be the key question.)

MBIA (after a puff from his pipe): Our ancestors used to say: 'The first day of the marriage is only the beginning of it!' Therefore . . . er . . .

(With calculated carelessness.)

I only brought two hundred thousand francs with me . . .

ALL (awe-striken): Two hundred thousand francs . . . two hundred thousand francs . . .

ABESSOLO (softly, to the others): Didn't I tell you?

MBIA: (with his usual modesty): I do realise it's only a small sum of money . . .

ALL (same as above): O o o oh . . .!

MBIA (same as above): But, as I was saying, it's only the beginning.

ATANGANA (eagerly): You're right! Marriage settled! Give me the money!

(MBIA gives the money to MBARGA, who counts it with ABESSOLO, then gives it to ATANGANA. The other villagers watch while carrying on with the conversation.)

MEZOE: What do I always say? There's nothing like secondary school for making girls valuable. Look at Juliette whom we were foolishly proposing to give to a mere farmer: she's now going to be the most important lady in Sangmélima!

ONDUA (softly): Is our son-in-law a bachelor then?

MEZOE (softly): Not quite, but he's only got eight wives. None of them ever went to secondary school like Juliette. She's the one who's going to rule that house, I can tell you that!

ATANGANA (straightening up): Yes, it's correct! Two hundred thousand francs!

MBIA (getting up): I must leave you now. I've got to attend a cocktail party

Act Two

at the Secretary of State's private residence this very evening . . .

(He is seen to the road by ANTANGANA and OYONO.)

MEZOE (scandalised): You see what I told you? Atangana's taking the great man away already! He wants to stop us asking him . . .

MBARGA (sulkily): Don't say anything! Just let's wait and see!

ABESSOLO (quickly): Ah Atangana! . . Atangana! . . . . Come back . . . Come back!

ATANGANA (returning with MBIA): What's the matter now?

ABESSOLO: You're asking *me*?

(Softly.)

Have we all told Mbia what he must bring us before he can have our daughter?

(Louder, to MBIA.)

Before you can have Juliette, you'll have to bring me three large loin-cloths like the ones the Bamileke traders sell in Zoetele: also, one whole sack of cola nuts from the North . . . a nice lawn chair . . .

(MBIA signals to ENGULU to take all this down.)

OYONO: I must have a brand new motor cycle . . .

MEZOE: For the time being, I'll be happy to have . . .

(He points at MBIA's own clothes.)

. . . a terylene suit!

ONDUA (thinking methodically): You'll bring me . . . er . . . a large iron bed, a cotton mattress, a big cupboard . . . ten cases of red wine, twenty bottles of . . .

MBARGA (impatiently): Yes . . . yes . . . It's all right, you drunk! Has the headman himself already spoken?

ALL: Mbarga must speak . . . yes . . . Mbarga must speak . . .

MBARGA (thundering): Just like you! Always leaving the greatest man in the village to speak last! Quiet!

(The villagers quieten down, and MBARGA turns slowly towards MBIA.)

As for me, I'm not saying anything yet! I'll come to see you in Sangmélima!

ATANGANA: Has everybody spoken? Good!

(To MBIA.)

I'll tell you what you must bring me to finish the marriage! I must have a radio-set, with gramophone . . .

OYONO (rushing to speak softly to his father): Ah Tita . . . Tita! . . . Better ask him to bring you a transistor radio!

ATANGANA (brushing him aside): Never such nonsense in my house! I won't have any of these tiny radio sets which always tell lies!

(With expressive gestures.)

What I want is a big, reliable set that can speak Bulu now and then . . .

ALL (approvingly): Yes . . . yes . . . Bulu . . . Bulu . . .a Bulu set . . .

ATANGANA (to MBIA): I'll carry on . . .

(ENGULU is still jotting it all down.)

One 'Hercules' bicycle . . .

(Softly to MBARGA.)

I'm told they're the most expensive machines on the market . . .

(Louder.)

Four terylene suits . . . five woollen blankets . . . a sewing machine with a pedal . . . ten large loin-cloths . . .

MBARGA (softly, to ATANGANA): I'm told he also runs a coach!

ATANGANA (softly, to MBARGA): Does he? Then we'll demand it when it's time to have the marriage registered!

(Louder, to MBIA.)

And for my wife, a complete set of kitchen ware, ten sacks of rice of one hundred kilogrammes each, and whatever she might like to ask for herself. But never forget to bring me four oxen, fifteen sheep, ten goats, twenty pigs . . .

ONDUA (softly, to ATANGANA, with an eloquent gesture): What do you think you're doing, Atangana? How can you forget the most important thing?

ATANGANA: Ah . . . yes! You must also bring us thirty cases of red wine . . .

ALL (praising ATANGANA's wisdom): Ya a a ah!

MBIA (straightening himself): Is that all?

(The villagers stare at each other in disbelief while ATANGANA is desperately trying to think of a few more things to ask for.)

ATANGANA: Er . . . er . . . I think that will do . . .

(He adds, because one never knows.)

for the moment!

MBIA: Good-bye then. Engulu!

ENGULU (following): Sah!

(They are seen out by ATANGANA. OYONO begins taking some of the unwanted chairs to the main house.)

MBARGA (accusingly): You saw that, didn't you? You saw what Atangana and his family just did?

Act Two

ABESSOLO (perplexed): What did we do?

MBARGA: You know very well that I've been trying to get a gun permit for the last four years, and you let your civil servant go without even mentioning that to him?

ABESSOLO (ruefully): Ah Oyônô! Go and tell your father to tell the great man . . .

MBARGA: I'll see the great man myself! I'll show you that I'm known everywhere!

ABESSOLO (apologetically): We didn't . . .

MBARGA: And I'll get my gun permit in spite of the jealousy of some people . . .

MEZOE: How are you going to do that?

MBARGA: Just you wait and see! I'll go and visit Mbia in Zoetele. Meanwhile, I'm going to ask him to come to my house for a couple of drinks . . .

ONDUA (speaking from experience): Whatever you do, don't let him know that you've got 'Arki' in your house!

MBARGA (scornfully): I've got nothing to fear! I'm not like you! *You're* one of these little people whom Medola, the police commissioner, keeps beating in Zoetele!

(He goes to the road.)

Come along, and you'll see how I entertain the great man in my house!

(MEZOE and ONDUA follow him. ABESSOLO goes to the main house while MAKRITA, BELLA, MATALINA and JULIETTE come from the kitchen. They come at the same time as ATANGANA who was returning from the road.)

MAKRITA: How did it go with the civil servant?

ATANGANA (satisfied with himself): Well . . . it all went very well indeed! The great man paid two hundred thousand francs, and . . .

(Beaming, to JULIETTE.)

Well, the marriage has been settled!

JULIETTE (furious): What? Settled? Do you really mean to ignore me when you make decisions affecting me? Couldn't you have consulted me? At least this once?

(All remain silent for a while. OYONO and MATALINA, who never went to secondary school, look at the elders, meaning: 'there's a secondary school girl for you!')

MATALINA: But he's a civil servant, Juliette! And a very wealthy man!

JULIETTE (getting angrier): I say I don't want to marry him! Besides, I've already told my mother that I'm engaged to someone else!

ATANGANA (who missed the last bit): And you dare to raise your voice when I'm speaking!

JULIETTE: I . . .

MAKRITA (appalled, running towards JULIETTE): Be quiet, Juliette! Your father's speaking!

ATANGANA (now looking for a scapegoat): That's the disgraceful behaviour you teach her!

(Calling the audience to witness.)

You listen to this: a very important civil servant wants to marry the girl who's supposed to be my daughter. He brings us many bottles of wine and beer . . .

OYONO (shaking his fist at JULIETTE): Wine and beer . . .

ATANGANA (same as above): He gives me two hundred thousand francs . . .

OYONO (same as above): Two hundred thousand francs . . .

ATANGANA (almost pleading with the audience): He doesn't speak to us like all great men do. Instead, he addressed us with respect!

(Proudly.)

Now we're all be entertained like white men at the 'Relais' whenever we go to Sangmélima. Many of us here in Mvoutessi will soon get gun permits and medals of honour. What's more important, I'll now be able to finish paying for the girl my son wants to marry in Ebolowa . . .

(Now that he has won his cause, he turns to JULIETTE and thunders.)

And you! You expect me to turn down all this just like that? You expect me to refuse to take so many riches just because . . .

(He mimics JULIETTE's voice.)

. . . You don't want to marry him!

(ABESSOLO bursts in. He looks angrily at the women present.)

ABESSOLO: I really can't understand you women!

(He pauses a little to catch his breath, and everybody thinks he is specifically referring to JULIETTE.)

What do you think you're doing? You leave me, an old man, to starve all day long in the village, and when you come back from the bush, you don't even think of getting me something to eat?

(BELLA goes to the kitchen. She will be heard pounding plantains later on.)

ATANGANA: Ah Tita'Abessôlô! Don't you know we've got lots of things going on here?

ABESSOLO (unconcernedly, going to his lawn chair): What things?

ATANGANA: You might never get your loin-cloths and your sacks of cola nuts after all.

Act Two

(Slowly.)

Juliette doesn't want to get married!

(ABESSOLO is so shocked he misses his chair, and falls on the floor.)

ABESSOLO: Hee Yeeaah! Didn't I warn you, Atangana? Didn't I warn you never to send your daughter to that school in Dibamba? You see what's happening now?

(Dolefully, to himself as he is resuming his seat.)

Yeeaah! my cola nuts! These missionaries came here to corrupt our land! They certainly taught Juliette to disobey her family!

MATALINA (who is now convinced that there is something wrong with her cousin): But think about it again, Juliette!

(Slowly.)

A civil servant . . . a car . . . many servants in the house . . . what more could any girl want?

JULIETTE (annoyed, at the top of her voice): I'm already engaged!

ATANGANA (jumps at hearing this): What, engaged?

(He comes closer.)

Will that man find three hundred thousand francs to pay back your first suitors?

(Distinctly.)

Three hundred thousand francs!

JULIETTE: He doesn't even have one franc! He's still studying in Yaoundé, at the Lycée Leclerc.

ALL (horrified): Hee yeeaah!

(OYONO who was going to the kitchen, rushes back and talks angrily to JULIETTE.)

OYONO: What? A schoolboy in our family? Never!

JULIETTE (defiantly): And why not?

OYONO: You're my sister!

JULIETTE: But . . .

OYONO: You know I need lots of money to pay for my future wife!

MAKRITA: Your brother's right, Juliette! Girls are very expensive in Ebolowa! He needs lots of money, and you belong to him!

JULIETTE: But I'm a free person!

OYONO (exasperated): A free person! Listen to that! A free person, after all the money we spent for her studies!

ATANGANA (bitterly): Five whole years in Dibamba! I spent all the money I got from my cocoa for her, and now that I've found the right man to pay me back . . .

JULIETTE (stubbornly): I love someone else!

MATALINA (incredulously): How could you do that, Juliette? A mere
schoolboy! Will he ever buy you expensive dresses? If at least he was
studying at the National School of Administration!

ATANGANA (who thinks there has been quite enough nonsense already):
You say that young man hasn't got any money?

JULIETTE: Not a franc!

ATANGANA (with a triumphant sneer): Then you'll marry Mbia!

(Clapping his hands.)

And that's final!!

(He goes towards the kitchen.)

JULIETTE (bursts into tears): I don't love him!

ATANGANA (from the doorstep): You'll love him! How insolent! You're
going to make me miss a medal!

(He goes in.)

MAKRITA (comfortingly): Don't annoy your father, Juliette! Do as he
says! You're going to make him miss a medal!

JULIETTE (still sobbing): You don't even listen to me! You don't love me!
Nobody loves me here!

ABESSOLO (who was moving to the kitchen): Shut up, you stupid thing!
Why do you think we're demanding such a high bride-price for you?
Doesn't that show how dearly we love you? *You're* the one who doesn't
love us! You don't love your brother . . .

JULIETTE (same as above): But I . . .

OYONO: Yes! You don't want me to get married!

BELLA (calling from the kitchen): What are you waiting for? The meal is
ready!

MAKRITA: Come, Juliette, let's go and eat! You've travelled a long way!
Your grandmother's calling us!

(She goes to the kitchen with MATALINA and OYONO. Various noises
are heard from inside; knives and forks, wailing of a greedy dog that has
just been kicked, elders scolding those children who don't eat properly,
and ATANGANA's angry exclamations as he comments on his daughter's
disgraceful behaviour. JULIETTE remains alone on stage for sometime,
obviously waiting for somebody. OKO appears some time afterwards,
reading as he walks. JULIETTE runs to him as soon as she sees him.)

JULIETTE (talking very excitedly): Oko! There you are at last!

(They embrace.)

Act Two

Just as I told you! The visit we wanted to pay to my family has been a disaster . . . a real disaster!

(She pauses.)

Would you imagine that they want me to get married?

(OKO does not seem terribly upset at hearing this. He is quite a nice fellow, although inevitably pompous, like a true sixth-former of the Lycée Leclerc where he has just started studying philosophy. He replies very calmly.)

OKO: I still can't see the disaster!

JULIETTE (put off by Oko's reaction): What? I tell you they say they want me to get married, and that's all you've got to say?

OKO (quietly): Isn't that what we were planning to do?

JULIETTE: That's exactly what you don't understand . . .

OKO (raising his hand in a 'don't get excited' way): I understand! Things are a bit more rushed than we expected, but after all, it might be better to get married now than later on, when we . . .

JULIETTE: I tell you you don't . . .

OKO (same as above): I do . . . I do . . . ! But I still think that since your parents are so understanding . . .

JULIETTE (angrily): You call that being understanding? Marrying me off like that!

OKO (conciliating): But isn't that a lot better than if they had opposed our marriage?

JULIETTE (sighing): That's where you're mistaken, Oko! My family want me to marry someone else!

OKO (startled: he suddenly forgets the part he was playing): What. Someone else? Whoever could that be?

JULIETTE (rather amused): Well . . . I only have to say yes, you know! For instance, there's a young farmer who came here and paid one hundred thousand francs to my family . . .

OKO (dismayed): What?

JULIETTE: And a great civil servant from Sangmélima who's promising everybody lots of things, gun permits and medals. Of course, they're all in favour of the civil servant . . .

OKO (stammering): And what about you, Juliette?

JULIETTE (offended): I beg . . .

OKO (quickly): Forgive me, Juliette! I think I no longer know what I'm saying . . . You were quite right: this is a disaster!

JULIETTE: I haven't told you the worst yet: the civil servant paid two

Three Suitors: One Husband

hundred thousand francs to my family this afternoon!

OKO (appalled): Two hundred . . . what?

JULIETTE: Two hundred thousand francs!

OKO: So much money?

JULIETTE: Yes!

(She pauses; they both think.)

You know, I wonder what would have happened if I didn't think of asking you to go and stay with my cousin Kouma until I'd had time to mention you to my family. By the way, where is Kouma? Didn't he promise to come with you to see me?

OKO: He should be here any moment now . . .

(Then, as the terrible situation occurs to him again, he says.)

What am I going to do now?

JULIETTE (hesitantly): Er . . . find the money to pay your rivals back, I guess . . .

OKO (bitterly): And as I am as poor as any self-respecting student . . .

JULIETTE: Things become somewhat difficult . . .

OKO (annoyed by JULIETTE's attitude): Come on, Juliette! You think it's just up to me to become rich overnight?

JULIETTE: Well . . . you could try and become at least three hundred thousand francs rich!

OKO (walking away from her in anger): And where do you expect me to find that kind of money?

JULIETTE (coming closer to him): Listen to me: you see that nobody's going to help us here . . .

OKO (gradually remembering his great philosopher's part): Nothing could be more obvious . . .

JULIETTE: And that we've got to find a way out . . .

OKO: A logical consequence . . .

JULIETTE (hesitantly): But I don't think you're going to like my suggestion.

OKO (puzzled): What is it?

JULIETTE (putting her arms around him): You promise you won't get angry?

OKO (putting his arms around her): Well . . . that's an easy thing to do!

JULIETTE (joyfully running to the main house): Good! I'll bring you three hundred thousand francs!

OKO (taken aback): What?

JULIETTE (stopping): You just promised!

Act Two

(OKO remains quiet.)

You're going to use the three hundred thousand francs which the farmer and the civil servant paid here to refund them.

OKO (startled): You mean we should steal that?

JULIETTE: Not at all! You're simply going to pay a bride-price for me by returning the money to the people to whom it actually belongs!

OKO (raising his arms in theatrical despair): Frankly, I don't know what philosopher to invoke now!

(With dignity.)

Juliette, you know very well that I . . .

JULIETTE (as an approaching moped is heard): Shut up! I can hear Kouma coming! You'll both wait for me here! Don't let anybody else see you!

(She goes in. KOUMA appears soon afterwards on his old moped. He stops the engine and begins talking as he parks his machine.)

KOUMA (softly): Where have you been, my friend? Isn't it rather imprudent of you to be hanging around here, especially now that I understand lots of things are going on?

OKO (moving towards KOUMA): You're right: it's not very prudent of me to be here.

KOUMA (begins pacing to and fro): We never expected this to happen!

(He sits down.)

You know, about half an hour ago, just after you'd left, I decided to go and greet my uncle Mbarga, the headman of Mvoutessi. You can very well imagine my surprise when I found a big car parked outside his house, and I was introduced to a civil servant and his driver who were drinking 'Arki' inside!

OKO: So they haven't gone yet?

KOUMA: Not yet! They still have quite a few bottles to empty, as a matter of fact. And the headman said to me: 'Come and greet Mbia, your brother-in-law! He's the great civil servant from Sangmélima who's just paid two hundred thousand francs for your cousin Juliette!'

OKO (speaking to himself): Two hundred thousand francs . . .

KOUMA: And I rushed back as soon as I could get away to try and catch up with you before you'd met Juliette.

(He pauses, and gets up.)

By the way, where is she?

OKO (indicating the main house): She's in that house.

KOUMA: Does she know you're waiting here, on the road?

OKO: I hope she still does!

Three Suitors: One Husband

KOUMA (surprised): Then what's she doing in there?

OKO: I wonder!

KOUMA: I'll go and look for her.

(He goes towards the main house.)

We simply must find a . . . Ah! There comes Juliette!

(JULIETTE has just come out of the main house with an old briefcase. She runs towards the two young men.)

JULIETTE: Oh! . . . Kouma is here too! Good! Now, listen to me, both of you: you've got three hundred thousand francs in this briefcase!

(KOUMA and OKO are too surprised to react.)

Come on, take!

KOUMA (looking at OKO): What does that mean?

JULIETTE: You'll soon understand! We want to play a good joke on all these people.

KOUMA (suspiciously): And the good joke is going to cost them . . .

JULIETTE: Not a franc.

KOUMA (surprised): But the money?

JULIETTE: Actually belongs to the people to whom you're going to pay it back.

OKO: Juliette, you know . . .

KOUMA (jumping in excitement): Come, Oko! I understand now!

(He pulls OKO by the hand.)

Come along! We're going to stage something simply great for them! Great! Nobody will ever know what it's all about! Since they only want to have wealthy men, we're going to bring them a very special suitor: the wealthiest man in the world!

OKO: The wealthiest man in the world? Who's that?

KOUMA (almost forcing him on the carrier of the moped): Come on, sit there, and you'll soon be a wealthy man! Marriage is an expensive business nowadays! Better take advantage of your money, and get married! Give me the briefcase, Juliette!

JULIETTE (giving him the briefcase): I'll come to see you as soon as we finish cooking the evening meal!

KOUMA (trying to start his engine): Yes, come, and we'll organise all that! We'll be off now. Cheerio, Juliette.

(To the audience.)

See you in the fifth act . . . !

Act Three

(He has now managed to start his old moped. They go off and the
curtain falls.)

ACT THREE

The same day at nightfall. We are inside MAKRITA's kitchen, which is lit
by a wood fire at the far end of the stage, and an old hurricane lamp. There
are some shelves filled to capacity with bowls, basins and plates of various
sizes, knives, forks, pots, etc, in the corner opposite to the fire. MAKRITA,
BELLA and JULIETTE are cooking the evening meal. BELLA is taking
peanuts out of an enormous basket set on a low table next to the shelves
containing kitchen ware. MAKRITA, who is cooking plantains, puts them
in a huge pot which is boiling over the fire as she peels them. JULIETTE is
now less smartly dressed than in the previous acts; she is sitting on a low
bamboo bed on the left, and cracking peanuts. MAKRITA is also sitting on
a similar bed placed near the fire. A third bed is placed on the right, where
BELLA will be sitting later on.

BELLA (having filled her basket): Now that we are all by ourselves,
  Juliette, I want you to explain to me your attitude. Why won't you
  marry the civil servant? He's so wealthy! Aren't you proud of such a
  suitor?

JULIETTE: No, Na' Bella!

BELLA (going to her bed): No? Did I hear you say no? How can you be so
  disobedient to your family? We had so much trouble bringing you up!

MAKRITA (without stopping peeling her plantains): So much trouble, my
  daughter! You can't imagine how difficult it was for your grandmother
  and me to persuade your father to give you some money whenever you
  were sent down from Dibamba because you hadn't paid all your fees.

BELLA (sitting down): Yes! My son had become the laughing stock of
  Mvoutessi! Everybody said it was very stupid of him to waste all the
  money he got from his cocoa on a mere daughter, instead of getting
  himself other wives . . .

MAKRITA: Or a wife for your brother . . .

BELLA: A wife for Oyônô! He wants to marry a nice, hard-working girl
  somewhere near Ebolowa.

Three Suitors: One Husband

JULIETTE (beginning to understand): And so . . .

MAKRITA: Well, I said to your brother: 'Don't worry about the bride-price you're asked to pay for your future wife! Your sister Juliette is attractive and she's been to secondary school! We'll be rich when some great man comes to marry her . . . '

BELLA: And that's exactly what has happened! Two suitors!

JULIETTE: I want neither of them! I told you so already!

MAKRITA (stopping for a moment): What? You mean you don't want your own brother to get married? You don't want your mother to have a daughter-in-law to help her grow peanuts and corn in the bush?

(Sighing.)

I think you simply haven't got a heart, Juliette! You . . .

(She is interrupted by MATALINA who is bringing two plates.)

MATALINA (cheerfully greeting them): Mbolo o! . . .

THE OTHERS: Mbolo o, Matalina!

MATALINA (going to sit next to JULIETTE): My mother sent you some food!

JULIETTE (taking the plates): Oh . . . thank you!

(She uncovers them.)

BELLA (touched): Monica never forgets her little Juliette! Never forgets the little child she used to carry on her back!

(To JULIETTE.)

Is it antelope meat she sent you?

JULIETTE (taking the plates to the shelves): I think so, Na' Bella!

(She puts them on the shelves.)

We'll eat that when we finish cooking.

MATALINA (helping crack the peanuts): We saved that piece of meat for the day you'd come back from Libamba.

MAKRITA (to JULIETTE who is returning to sit down): A big antelope got caught in one of your uncle Ondua's traps two weeks ago.

BELLA: And he sold all the meat! Sold it all to get more wine! More wine to . . .

(She claps her hands in indignation.)

Hee yeeaah! I never saw such a drunkard! To think he's my own son!

(Smiling to JULIETTE.)

When you go to live in that big house in Sangmélima, be sure to send your uncle Ondua a few bottles of red wine now and then . . .

JULIETTE (annoyed, at the top of her voice): I'm not going to Sangmélima!

Act Three

MAKRITA (frightened): Not so loud! Your father might hear you!

MATALINA: But, Juliette! How could a girl refuse to marry a man who loves her enough to pay two hundred thousand francs for her? Other men couldn't have paid that much, you know!

JULIETTE: Does money prove love?

MAKRITA (covering her pot): How could a man prove it otherwise?

JULIETTE: I've told you my fiancé hasn't got any money, and yet I'm sure he loves me.

MATALINA (sneering at such naivety): You're sure he loves you? What has he given you already?

(The following questions are asked very quickly.)

BELLA: How many dresses?

JULIETTE: No dresses!

MATALINA: And you love him?

MAKRITA: Has he got a car?

MATALINA: Does he make a lot of money?

JULIETTE: He . . .

BELLA: Has he got a large house?

MATALINA: Does he work with the Government?

BELLA: Can he . . .

JULIETTE (getting impatient): Nothing of the sort!

BELLA (after a pause): And whereabouts is that young man from?

JULIETTE: From Ambam!

THE OTHERS (appalled): Eeaaah!

BELLA: From so far away? You want to leave us?

JULIETTE (smiling): Were you born in Mvoutessi, Grandmother?

MATALINA (scornfully): And just what is so charming about him?

JULIETTE: Nothing! I love him!

BELLA (indignantly): You must be out of your mind, Juliette! Since when do girls fall in love without the permission of their families? How can you disappoint us all like that?

(She gets up and walks towards JULIETTE.)

I tell you again, my child, you must marry a great man! It's about time you too began bringing us food, drinks, and other things from the city like Cécilia's been doing ever since she's been living with her European in Mbalmayo! It's about time we too became respectable people!

JULIETTE (amused): Respectable? What do you . . .

MATALINA (struck by a new idea): You know what I've been thinking, Juliette? Since you don't want to get married, why not go and get yourself a good job in a big Government office?

(Confidentially.)

Everybody says it's not at all difficult for attractive girls!

(Excitedly.)

Then we'd all be coming now and then to see you and spend a few months in the city like everybody else!

JULIETTE: Why don't *you* go and get yourself a job in the city, if it's so easy?

(MATALINA is hurt by this reply. She gets up abruptly and says to BELLA who was still standing at the centre of the kitchen.)

MATALINA: I'd better go back home now, Na' Bella! It's getting darker and darker.

BELLA (comfortingly, walking her to the door): Yes, my child! Go and join your mother Monica! She must be feeling lonely in the house, with your father still drinking at the headman's house!

(MATALINA goes out, and BELLA turns to JULIETTE.)

I'm beginning to think you'll never listen to us, Juliette!

JULIETTE (pleading): You just don't understand me! . . . I . . .

MAKRITA (in a sad, disappointed voice): She'll never be the obedient daughter I'd always hoped she would! For instance, I'm sure that once she's married to that civil servant, she'll always keep him from giving her relatives all that they'll demand on top of the bride-price!

(She begins to remove the plantain peels from the floor, putting them in a waste basket.)

She'll be cutting down on the expenses, instead of threatening her husband with divorce whenever he refuses to satisfy us! I can just see her now, offering one small glass of wine only to her uncles, instead of five or six large bottles to every one of them!

BELLA (sitting down at her usual place): Or perhaps she'll . . .

MAKRITA: (straightening up): I know the disgraceful way these girls of today usually treat their relatives in Sangmélima! Whenever we go to see her, Juliette will certainly send us away after three weeks only, pretending that food is expensive in the city!

JULIETTE (who can't help laughing): Is that why everybody in this village wants me to marry the civil servant?

MAKRITA (annoyed by JULIETTE's laughter): Of course! Don't you know that all the men in Mvoutessi envy Meka, Cécilia's father, whenever his daughter sends workmen from Mbalmayo to clear his cocoa plantation for him?

Act Three

(Men's voices are heard from outside.)

BELLA: Oh . . ! Your father and your grandfather are back from the headman's house Juliette! Quick! Go and light the big pressure lamp before my son begins shouting!

(JULIETTE gets up as ATANGANA is in fact beginning to shout.)

ATANGANA (from outside): Where's my big lamp? . . . Where are the women of this village? . . . Ah Makrita! . . . Makrita!

MAKRITA: ou-ou-ou-ou!

ATANGANA: Where's my big lamp?

MAKRITA: The big lamp is coming!

ATANGANA: Quick! I've got other visitors! Ndi's just come!

JULIETTE (as she was about to go out): Ndi?

BELLA: Yes, Ndi! The first of your suitors. He promised to come tonight.

(Confidentially.)

But if you ask me, he'll have to step aside for your civil servant! Go and light the big lamp, my child!

(JULIETTE goes out. Blackout. Then the lights come on again, dimly at first. ATANGANA, ABESSOLO, OYONO and NDI are seen outside the main house, at the usual place. The lighting will become more intense when JULIETTE comes out with the big pressure lamp. She sets it on the floor, in the middle of the stage, then she hesitates, wondering whether she should greet NDI. NDI is somewhat blinded by the intense lamp light at first; but, as soon as he recognises JULIETTE, he strides in her direction as boldly as any man who, having paid one hundred thousand francs for a woman feels he is fully entitled to embrace her. But JULIETTE runs to the safety of the kitchen like a frightened antelope. NDI is rather disconcerted, and he stops on the spot while the other men look at him with eloquent smiles meaning: 'Serves you right! You wouldn't listen to us! We warned you, etc.')

ATANGANA (rather uneasily): I tell you again, Ndi; it's all Juliette's fault! She doesn't want to marry you. You see she's crazy about a certain civil servant, and that man has already paid us a bride-price of two hundred thousand francs.

ABESSOLO (contentedly): He'll also bring me sacks of cola nuts from the north!

NDI (bewildered): But I paid you one hundred thousand francs!

ATANGANA (shrugging like a man sure of his position): Well, it's up to you: you can either be refunded . . .

OYONO (snappishly): Or imprisoned!

NDI (frightened): But why?

ATANGAN: Don't you understand? The man we're talking about is the one who rules everybody in Sangmélima! He even speaks to the Secretary of State like you speak to me!

OYONO: And he never goes anywhere without at least two hundred thousand francs in his pocket . . .

NDI (giving up like a quiet, law-abiding young man): In that case, I'd rather have my money back, and return to Awae!

ATANGANA (delightedly, going to the main house): I won't be long . . . I wont be long . . .

(He goes in.)

ABESSOLO (comfortingly, to NDI who is deeply reflecting on the vanity of human wishes): You're a very wise young man, my son! It's not always easy to get back the money paid in such cases!

(Confidentially.)

Besides, going about with an attractive wife today . . .

(He is interrupted by MBARGA and MEZOE who rush in, exclaiming and raising their hands in shocked surprise.)

MEZOE (moving towards a vacant seat): Just what I always say! These children of today are corrupt . . . useless!

MBARGA (clapping his hands): This is incredible! . . . Hee yeeaah!

ABESSOLO: What is it?

MBARGA (disgustedly, sitting down): Don't even ask me, Abessôlô! Young people who dare to eat a viper − Belinga and Owônô it was − without the permission of the elders of this village!

(ABESSOLO is about to exclaim but MBARGA leans forward so as to let him know that he hasn't heard the worst bit yet.)

A real viper, big, fat . . . a viper!

(He pauses.)

And all they saved for us was three quarters of the meat!

ABESSOLO (raising his hands to his head in despair): Hee yeeaah! Only three quarters of the meat!

MEZOE: Three quarters!

(The three of them begin cursing the younger generation. Meanwhile ATANGANA, who has discovered the theft, appears on the doorstep of the main house. He makes frantic gestures at OYONO to try and take NDI away.)

OYONO: Come along, Ndi! I saved a whole calabash of palm wine for you in my uncle Ondua's house, down the road!

(He leads the way.)

Real palm wine, not at all like the milk I once drank in your house in Awae!

Act Three

(They go away, and ATANGANA joins the others on stage.)

ATANGANA (trying to keep his voice down): Everything's lost! Lost! They've left nothing . . . nothing!

ABESSOLO (echoing ATANGANA): Nothing . . . nothing except three quarters!

ATANGANA (surprised): What do you mean, they left three quarters? I tell you they took everything!

MEZOE (jumping up): What? They've now taken everything?

ATANGANA: Everything!

MEZOE (longing for action): Ah Mbarga! What did I tell you? We must put both of them flat on the floor, and give them a sound spanking!

ATANGANA (eagerly, with rising hopes): So you know who did it?

MBARGA: Have you ever seen the headman of Mvoutessi paralysed by any situation?

ATANGANA (moving towards MBARGA): Who are they?

ABESSOLO (scornfully): Who else could they be, except the children *you* raise today, Belinga and Owono?

ATANGANA (shocked): These two good-for-nothings? How could they . . .

ABESSOLO (same as above): Haven't I always told you that in my day . . .

ATANGANA: And you say they left three quarters of it?

MEZOE (who hasn't yet forgotten about the spanking): Only three quarters!

ATANGANA (clapping his hands): Zua Meka! I hope that's going to be enough for Ndi!

ABESSOLO (scandalised): What, for Ndi? So you're the ones who teach your sons such behaviour?

ATANGANA (perplexed): Teach them what?

ABESSOLO (accusingly): It's you! They've already taken everything except three quarters of the meat! Now, instead of saving that for the elders of Mvoutessi, you say you want to give it to some stranger from Awae?

ATANGANA (more and more perplexed): But since . . .

ABESSOLO (picking up his fly-whisk): I don't want any more of it! You'll eat your viper all by yourselves!

ATANGANA (staring at the others): Our viper?

ABESSOLO (going to the main house): And never call me again when there are important things to be discussed in this village!

MBARGA: Ah Abessôlô!

ABESSOLO (from the doorstep): I don't . . .

MBARGA: Don't go away! A true sage never gets angry when foolish people

Three Suitors: One Husband

are speaking! Look at me: am I getting angry?

ABESSOLO (coming back): What's the world coming to? Ah Atangana! Have you forgotten that vipers are taboo animals, to be eaten only by the elders of the village?

ATANGANA (who no longer hopes to understand): Haven't I . . .

ABESSOLO: Then why do you want to give our viper to Ndi?

ATANGANA (exasperated): Who wants to give your viper to Ndi?

ABESSOLO: What have you just said?

ATANGANA: I was talking about my money: my three hundred thousand francs!

ABESSOLO (in a worried voice): What happened to your money?

ATANGANA (distinctly): It has been stolen!

ALL (simultaneously): Hee yeeaah!

MBARGA: Whoever could have done that?

ATANGANA: Haven't you just said . . .

ABESSOLO (quickly): That was something more important: a viper!

ATANGNA: Then I'm really lost! How am I going to pay back Ndi? Or else, what am I going to give to Mbia?

MEZOE (terrified): Yeeaah! Mbia! The great man who controls the police commissioners of the prison!

(They look at one another in silent grief for quite a while.)

MBARGA (suddenly brightening up): Listen to me! Why don't we ask Ndi to pay us that money? If he agrees to pay us the civil servant's two hundred thousand francs, we'll give him Juliette right away! It would be much wiser to try to come to an agreement between villagers, without the great people of the city hearing about the matter!

ALL (with some relief): Mbarga speaks the truth!

ATANGANA (going to the road): Ah Oyônô! Come, you and your brother-in-law!

(While they wait for NDI and OYONO, the men on stage try to put on more cheerful countenances. ABESSOLO even lights his pipe again.)

NDI (who is slightly tipsy): Good . . . good . . . it's all right with me! I'll take my money!

(There are disapproving grunts.)

And you can keep your daughter! On second thoughts I'd rather have a less educated wife! Perhaps she'd be more submissive!

(He moves towards ATANGANA while reaching out his hand. ATANGANA casts a desperate glance at MBARGA who replies with a wink meaning: don't worry! I'll take care of him myself!)

Act Three

MBARGA (with conviction): Ndi speaks the truth! What's the matter with the men of Mvoutessi? Since when do sensible villagers prefer civil servants to farmers? How could you have rejected my son Ndi? A nice, considerate young man who'd never see me in Awae without offering me lots of 'Atki' to drink!

ATAⁿGANA (ruefully): Forgive us. Ah Mbarga! We know nothing!

(NDI, who suspects some change in the general situation, turns round and looks at MBARGA.)

MBARGA (not unaware of the effect of his speech): Nobody else will marry Juliette!

(To NDI himself.)

Er . . . tell me, my son: I was a very good friend of your late father's wasn't I?

NDI (staring): My late father? Which one?

MBARGA: Your own father! Don't you remember?

NDI: But . . .

MBARGA (quickly): Ah . . . I see!

(To the others.)

My son was still a mere baby when his father died!

(Pretending to cry.)

Yeeaah! What a man that was! Hee yeeaah . . . !

NDI (as the others are joining MBARGA in mourning the dead man): My father isn't dead yet!

(MBARGA and the other mourners are put off for a moment, then the headman says with as much confidence as possible.)

MBARGA: Isn't he . . . ? Oh . . . ! Then embrace me, my son!

(He embraces NDI.)

Ah Abessôlô! What did I tell you yesterday? A great man like my son's father couldn't have died just like that! Who's greater than him in Awae?

ALL: Who else!

MBARGA (shouting): Ah Oyônô! Don't just stand there looking at me! Go and get a big armchair for my son-in-law?

(OYONO rushes to the main house, and MBARGA carries on with authority.)

He'll marry Juliette! Don't let me hear any more nonsense in this village about the civil servant!

(Another pause. OYONO is bringing out the same armchair in which MBIA was sitting at the beginning of the second act. MBARGA asks him to set it exactly in the same position in the centre of the stage, and everybody present almost forces a bewildered NDI to sit down. MBARGA then carries on just as he was doing in the second act.)

MBARGA: Ndi will have our daughter! What can civil servants do for you? Would they help you clear a patch of land for your plantations?

ALL: Never!

MBARGA: Would they ever raise the price of your cocoa?

ALL: Tee keeaah!

MBARGA: Would a civil servant bring you something to drink?

ALL (sincerely): Never! Ndi must have Juliette!

MBARGA (to NDI who is now filled with gratitude): You see, Ndi? This is the way *I* settle marriage questions in Mvoutessi! All you need is to be loved by the family of the girl you want! You'll be our son-in-law . . . if you wish so, of course!

NDI (eagerly, getting up): But I'm asking for nothing else!

MBARGA (casually): Then pay the civil servant his two hundred thousand francs!

NDI (hoping he didn't hear right): Pay what?

MBARGA: The civil servant's money: two hundred thousand francs!

NDI (beginning to understand): And where do you expect me to find that kind of money? You want me to steal?

MBARGA (imprudently): And what if you did? We too have had our money stolen!

ALL (disapprovingly): Aah ka, Mbarga!

NDI (furious): So it's like that? You've been robbed, and you're trying to rob me too!

(Going from one person to the other.)

Give me back my money!

OYONO (insolently, now that there is nothing to lose): And if we refuse?

NDI (exasperated): What, refuse? Then I'll go to Zoételé to see the police!

ABESSOLO (collapsing on the floor, away from NDI): Yeeaah! I'm a dead man! . . . I'm a dead man!

MBARGA (threateningly, to NDI): Did you come all the way from Awae to kill people here in Mvoutessi?

NDI (stunned): I kill people?

MBARGA (pointing at ABESSOLO on the floor): Haven't you just killed him with your witchcraft?

NDI: But . . .

(MEZOE and OYONO move threateningly in his direction, and he runs

Act Three

away, saying.)

You'll have to pay me back, I tell you! I'm going to Zoételé to see the police!

ATANGANA (scared): Ah Mbarga! What am I going to do? You're the one who knows Medola, the police commissioner of Zoételé!

MBARGA (quickly): Let's try the civil servant before he goes away! You remember we left him drinking in my house! *He* could easily pay back Ndi!

ABESSOLO (jumping up): And he could also imprison that . . .

MEZOE: Let him come!

ATANGANA: Ah Oyônô! Run and call the civil servant!

OYONO (running to the road): Oh . . . there he is, about to get into his car!

(He disappears, and is heard shouting.)

Wait . . . wait!

MEZOE: He must come! We'll ask him to pay us the money and take Juliette away this very evening! He can always bring me the terylene suit I asked for later!

ATANGANA (firmly): Yes, he'll take her away if he pays the money! I'll bind Juliette hand and foot myself if necessary!

ABESSOLO: As soon as he gets here, Mbarga will . . .

MBARGA: Nonsense! Atangana himself must speak to the civil servant! After all, *he* lost the money!

ATANGANA (angrily): But haven't I told you that . . .

MEZOE: Quiet! Here comes the civil servant!

(MBIA and ENGULU come in, preceded by OYONO. MBIA is not walking too steadily: it is obvious that the headman has not been mean with his 'Arki'. MBARGA comes forward, timidly trying to take MBIA to the armchair, but MBIA brushes him aside with visible impatience, and remains standing.)

MBIA (sharply): Well? . . . What is it?

ATANGANA (looking for words): We . . . er . . . you were leaving already, were you?

MBIA: Of course!

MEZOE: For Yaoundé?

MBIA (impatiently): I told you so already! Why did you call me back?

MBARGA (insidiously): We thought you wouldn't mind taking Juliette with you!

MBIA (suddenly softened): Oh . . . would you like me to . . . I mean, would you let me do that?

ATANGANA (same as above): Well . . . er . . . you see . . .

(Trying to gain time.)

Ah Oyônô! Go and catch my big ram for your brother-in-law!

(OYONO goes out. Everybody waits for ATANGANA to carry on.)

MBIA (after an uneasy pause): You were saying . . .

ATANGANA: Well, as I was saying, we in Mvoutessi don't like to keep two things at the same time, the money and the woman for whom the money has been paid. One never knows these days! Poor Atemeteme in Ngolebang, for instance . . . Did you hear about that, Mbarga?

MBARGA (impatiently): Go on! Tell Mbia what we decided!

ATANGANA (hurriedly): Good! I like to speak like a real man! You pay me another one hundred thousand francs, and the marriage is settled!

MBIA (jumping): What? Another one hundred thousand francs?

ATANGANA (already retreating): Only that much . . .

MBARGA (trying to sound calm and dignified): And I see to it that the marriage certificate is signed!

MBIA (thundering): You want me to pay three hundred thousand francs for one woman only? Who do you think you are?

ABESSOLO: I . . . we . . .

MBIA (sharply, reaching out his hand): Enough! My money!

ALL: Hee yeeaah!

MBIA: My money I say!

(The villagers look at one another in dismay.)

Ha . . . I see! You want to rob me so your own sons can get married! Just you wait!

(Thundering to his servant.)

Engulu!

ENGULU (rushing forward): Sah?

MBIA (pacing to and fro like a big boss in his office): Take me the name of this village in your note-book!

(ENGULU takes out his note-book with official coolness. He begins writing without a glance at the terrified villagers.)

ENGULU (at the top of his voice, while writing): Name of this village in the note-book . . .

MBIA (same as above): Write that the people of this village have no respect for important civil servants like . . .

(Pointing at himself.)

. . . like me!

Act Three

ALL: Eeeaa keeaah!

ENGULU (same as above): No respect for important civil servants like . . .

(Stops and points at himself.)

. . . like me!

MBIA (same as above): Write also that the roads leading to Mvoutessi are poorly kept, and that the houses haven't been whitewashed in expectation of the honour of my visit . . .

ALL: Yeeaah!

ENGULU (same as above): Houses poorly kept . . . no whitewashed roads . . .

MBIA (same as above): The women of this village are illegally distilling 'Arki'! I drank . . .

(Quickly correcting himself.)

er . . . I saw some of it . . .

(He stops and turns towards his servant.)

You'll take it down correctly, won't you?

(Indicating his eyes.)

'Saw' . . . but not . . .

(Indicating his mouth.)

. . . 'Drank', some of it, . . .

(Now accusingly pointing at Mbarga.)

. . . in the Headman Mbarga's house!

MBARGA (appalled): Yeeaah! . . . Tita!

ENGULU (same as above): 'Arki' . . .

(Indicating his mouth.)

. . . 'drunk' . . . but not . . .

(Indicating his eyes.)

. . . 'seen' . . . in Headman Mbarga's house!

MBIA (after enjoying the effect produced): I'll send . . .

(Counting aloud to himself.)

. . . two . . . four . . . no . . . eight . . . er . . .

(Fortissimo.)

ten police commissioners here to-morrow!

ALL: Hee yeeaah! This is death!

ENGULU (same as above): . . . Eight . . . ten non-police commissioners to-morrow.

MBIA (moving to the road): And now, en route!

(Thundering.)

Engulu!

ENGULU (quietly noting): En route . . .

(Yelling.)

Sah!

(They go to the road, leaving the villagers in dismay.)

ATANGANA: I'm lost, lost! Two jail threats on the same day! That important man offended! If I only knew who stole my money!

(All, except MBARGA, begin moaning about these events.)

MBARGA (who had been thinking): Listen to me! Don't all begin crying like a crowd of women! You must behave like men!

ATANGANA (no longer venturing to hope): Speak, ah Mbarga!

MBARGA: Would such things ever have happened in the days of our ancestors?

ALL (firmly): Never!

MBARGA: Didn't the white men only come to spoil our land?

ALL (disgustedly): Ah ka ka ka!

MBARGA: Ah Abessôlô!

ABESSOLO: Here I am!

MBARGA: What did our ancestors used to say about the chameleon and the grey lizard?

ABESSOLO: 'When the chameleon dies, the grey lizard should inherit his sack of cola nuts . . . '

MBARGA (looking at the others in turn): Who's the grey lizard? Who should inherit the cola nuts? Who should be the leader here?

ALL: Only you!

MBARGA (confidentially): We could once discover the unknown! . . . Shouldn't we now send for a . . . a witch-doctor?

ALL (approvingly): A witch doctor . . . ! A witch-doctor!

MBARGA: Yes, we need a witch-doctor! You know that Sanga-Titi, the great witch-doctor, is somewhere near Mfouladja. Let's send Kouma there to ask him to come.

ALL (with suddenly regained hope): Ya a a ah!

MBARGA (getting up): He must perform here this very night! Ah Atangana! Be sure to have ready the things which you'll give him as presents: sheep, goats, anything witch-doctors usually demand before beginning to perform . . .

(He moves towards the road.)

Act Four

I'm now going to send Kouma to Mfouladja . . . He's the one with the motor-bike . . .

(He goes out, followed by MEZOE.)

ATANGANA (as he and the others move to the main house, taking the kerosene lamp and some of the chairs): Hee yeeaah! Ah Zua Meka! What a day!

(The curtain falls as they go in.)

ACT FOUR

The same place at night. The stage is now lit by the witch-doctor's red fire. All the villagers, male and female, stand in circle behind SANGA-TITI, the witch-doctor and his ASSISTANT who are seen dancing when the curtain rises. The WITCH-DOCTOR begins by playing a theme on his harp ('Mvet'), then he sings the solo part of the melody. The rest of the actors, and even those members of the audience who can do so, sing the chorus, and clap their hands rhythmically. As soon as the drummers begin playing their instruments, the WITCH-DOCTOR and his ASSISTANT begin dancing the 'Nyeng' — they are, on the whole, far better dancers than ONDUA in the second act — and asking other people from the cast or the audience to join in. The same will be repeated whenever dancing sequences are indicated in the text, as the whole act is primarily meant to be a dancing interlude.

ATANGANA (when the dancing has ceased): So sit down, Witch-doctor! I asked you to come to my house because . . .

SANGA-TITI (sharply interrupting him): Leave it all to me! I know what you want to say already!

(The villagers are impressed. MBARGA looks at the audience and says proudly.)

MBARGA: You see? It takes a great man like me to find such a competent witch-doctor!

ATANGANA (excitedly): Good . . . good . . . ! But please hurry! I seem to see these police commissioners of Zoételé and Sangmélima coming to arrest me!

SANGA-TITI (quietly sitting down): You know what our ancestors used to say: 'dead men never speak unless it has rained . . . '

Three Suitors: One Husband

ATANGANA: Ah Oyônô! Go and catch me the ram we saved for the witch-doctor!

(OYONO goes out.)

SANGA TITI: You're a wise man!

(He begins playing another theme on his 'Mvet'. The villagers sing the chorus and clap their hands, but there is no dancing this time. Meanwhile, the ASSISTANT is busy displaying various items: mirrors, antelope horns, etc, in front of SANGA-TITI's seat. The WITCH-DOCTOR stops as soon as his ASSISTANT is ready.)

SANGA-TITI: Where are all the people of this village?

ATANGANA: Come, all of you! We've got to find out who stole my money!

(The villagers move closer to the WITCH-DOCTOR's fire.)

SANGA-TITI (after duly consulting his mirrors): My mirrors tell me that you're looking for a certain sum of money. Am I mistaken?

ALL (amazed): Hee yeeaah! He knows what it's all about!

ATANGANA (eagerly, he is confident now): Yes! I've had a large sum of money stolen! Three hundred thousand francs! I received that money as a bride-price for my daughter . . .

SANGA-TITI (with authority): Be quiet! I'll tell you everything! You've lost a sum of three hundred thousand francs!

ALL (same as above): He found out the amount of money missing!

SANGA-TITI: You received that money as a bride-price for your daughter!

ALL: What a great witch-doctor!

SANGA-TITI: I could easily tell you who stole that money. But . . .

(As they look at him questioningly.)

Well . . . you know, when a river has dried up, the water no longer runs!

ATANGANA: Ah Makrita! Go and get the duck they gave you in Ngolebang!

(MAKRITA goes out. SANGA-TITI consults his mirrors again.)

SANGA-TITI: Where is the headman of this village?

MBARGA (majestically straightening himself): Here I am!

SANGA-TITI: We'll start with you! Come and sit down there!

MBARGA (softly, to the audience): What did I tell you this afternoon? The headman should always come first!

(He goes and sits in front of the WITCH-DOCTOR.)

SANGA-TITI (looking into his antelope horn): How many wives have you got?

MBARGA (counting on his fingers and softly calling the names of some of his wives): Cécilia . . . Odilia . . . Martina . . . Ada . . . Akamba . . .

Act Four

(Louder.)

Twelve wives, officially married!

SANGA-TITI (suspiciously): That's not all!

MBARGA (a little disconcerted): What? . . . Ah yes! There's another woman I'm proposing to marry in Ngoantet!

SANGA-TITI: Just what I thought! My fetishes never tell lies!

(A pause, then he utters a cry of terror as he looks into his antelope horn again.)

Yeeaah! What do I see, Mbarga? Haven't you ever noticed anything unusual in this village?

MBARGA (upset): Unusual?

SANGA-TITI: Haven't you been taken ill?

MBARGA: Yes, witch-doctor! Many times!

SANGA-TITI: And you never worried about that?

MBARGA: They told me when I was at the hospital . . .

SANGA-TITI: (sharply) At the hospital! You shouldn't have gone there in the first place! Nobody likes you in this village!

(He leans forwards and adds.)

Especially now that the Government has promised to grant you a gun permit! Your life is in danger!

MBARGA (frightened, to MEZOE): What did I tell you, Mezôé?

(To the WITCH-DOCTOR.)

You say my life is in danger, witch-doctor?

SANGA-TITI: In real danger!

(He sits back again.)

Of course, I can't speak with empty hands!

MBARGA: A Mezôé! Go and tell my wife Akoudou to send me my black cockerel, the one they sent me from Akonolinga.

(MEZOE hurries out.)

Speak, witch-doctor!

SANGA-TITI (in an inspired voice): I am Sanga-Titi, the great witch-doctor who inherited the secrets of the past. Ah Mbarga, other people call you a wise man, but I say you're only a fool, because you've got no more than two eyes! To prove what I say, I'll ask you: where is your great-great-grandfather?

MBARGA (surprised): In the land of the dead, witch-doctor . . .

SANGA-TITI: Is he? Good. And what about your great-grandfather?

MBARGA: Long since dead, too.

Three Suitors: One Husband

SANGA-TITI: In brief, where are your ancestors? Where are all the great men of the past?

MBARGA: Dead, all of them.

SANGA-TITI (after checking the information with his mirrors): Dead, you said?

MBARGA (trying not to sound too positive about this): Dead.

SANGA-TITI: And you've never wondered what could have killed so many people? You never bothered to find out the cause of so many deaths in your village?

MBARGA (uneasily): As a matter of fact . . .

SANGA-TITI: Be quiet! I'll ask you something else: didn't you mourn anybody in this village last year?

MBARGA: We did!

SANGA-TITI (reproachfully): People keep dying in your village, you're the headman, and you simply don't worry about such disasters?

MBARGA: I've always thought that they were dying of some sort of disease . . .

SANGA-TITI: And where exactly does that disease usually come from?

MBARGA: We also mourned a lorry driver who died of an accident at the saw mill . . .

SANGA-TITI: And where exactly did that accident come from?

(Getting up, to the audience.)

Listen to me, all of you! Do you want to know why people die in this village? They die because the village is corrupt! Great people like your ancestors were couldn't have died without a cause! Accidental deaths are even hardly acceptable, otherwise, where are the great men of the past, who died before the white men had brought us accidents and hospitals?

(To the villagers in particular.)

Why aren't your ancestors still alive? Because they're dead, and the proof is that they're no longer alive!

(A pause. The villagers are highly impressed. There is an excited chatter while SANGA-TITI is looking into his antelope horn before proceeding.)

SANGA-TITI: Don't ask me to raise your ancestors from the dead! You may well believe that they'd rather stay where they are. Besides, supposing they were to come back, wouldn't you have to share your own cocoa plantations with them? And yet, you're now complaining about the Government taxes, and the Police commissioners of Zoételé keep beating you because you can't manage to pay them! On the other hand, supposing you were to follow your ancestors in the land of the dead, as so many of you have already foolishly done, you wouldn't be any richer, because you haven't got any cocoa plantations there. I'll therefore ask you: would you really like to die?

Act Four

ALL (like one man): Noo o! Tea keeaah!

SANGA-TITI (proud of his performance): You speak first, and I'll speak!

(He sits down.)

You show me whether you're really anxious to save your own village!

(SANGA-TITI begins playing a theme on his 'Mvet'. Singing and dancing begins as indicated at the beginning of the act. Those villagers who are not dancing or singing gather around MBARGA for a consultation. MEZOE comes back with the cockerel. MBARGA takes it, speaks softly to MEZOE who hurries out again. The WITCH-DOCTOR signals to the musicians to stop. He sits down, and MBARGA takes the cockerel to him.)

MBARGA: Witch-doctor! I'd like you to purify this village! I've had two more rams caught for you!

SANGA-TITI: You're a very wise man!

(He signals to his ASSISTANT to take the cockerel, and put it in a corner. Then he consults his mirrors again while MBARGA is sitting down.)

SANGA-TITI: Is there any of your wives you love more than the others?

MBARGA (rather embarrassed): Well . . .

SANGA-TITI: Never mind, never mind! My fetishes will tell me!

(A pause.)

Do you sometimes hear owls hooting around your villages at night?

ALL: We always hear them!

SANGA-TITI: Do you also hear chimpanzees howling in the forest at night two or three days before somebody dies here in Mvoutessi?

ALL (approvingly): Yeeaah! We always hear them!

SANGA-TITI (to everybody in a deep, frightening voice): This village is corrupt! The owls and the chimpanzees you hear at night are no ordinary birds or animals: they represent the evil spirits of the past, the same that killed your ancestors! Beware, all of you! Before I go, I'll sell you powerful fetishes to keep these evil spirits away from you! I'll also sell you some special preparations to protect you from death!

ALL (delightedly): Ya a a ah!

SANGA-TITI: Yes, don't forget to buy them tomorrow morning! Also, I must warn you against another great danger, especially for the men: take care whenever you go to another tribe to marry a new woman. Some of them bring powerful fetishes along because their mothers say to them: 'Take this or this, and you'll be sure to win your husband's heart, and bear him many children, and beat all your rivals in beauty, charm and housekeeping'. So your wives usually bring many dangerous fetishes when they come to this village! And I tell you again, such things can easily kill married men!

Three Suitors: One Husband

ALL THE MEN (horrified): Heee yeeaaah!

(As they shake threatening fists at the women, the WITCH-DOCTOR quickly adds.)

SANGA-TITI: Of course, this applies mainly to those of you who have many wives!

MBARGA (frightened): What can we do about that?

SANGA-TITI: Don't worry! I'll take care of that! For the time being, let's come back to the theft! Who's the chief of this house?

ATANGANA (taking MBARGA's place): Here I am!

SANGA-TITI: You say you've had your money stolen?

ATANGANA: Yes!

SANGA-TITI: How do you know?

ATANGANA (vindictively): Witch-doctor, if you only knew how the people of this village all hate my family! All this because I sent my daughter Juliette to secondary school! They . . .

SANGA-TITI (sharply): Be quiet! I'm better qualified than anyone else to know the truth! Nothing is impossible to my science! But I must have something for my trouble!

ATANGANA: You'll have anything you like! Just speak!

SANGA-TITI (consulting his mirrors): Didn't you go to Sangmélima two days ago to sell your cocoa?

ATANGANA (surprised): It's almost a week now!

SANGA-TITI (thundering): Two days ago! How dare you contradict me?

ALL (quickly): Ah Atangana! Listen to the witch-doctor! You know nothing! You went there two days ago! We saw you!

ATANGANA (perplexed): It must be two days ago then!

SANGA-TITI (triumphantly): You see? My fetishes never tell lies! So, while you were being paid the money for your ten sacks of cocoa . . .

ATANGANA (imprudently): I only sold three sacks . . .

SANGA-TITI (pretending to leave): You're much too . . .

ATANGANA (ruefully): Don't go, witch-doctor! I'll have two goats and a ram caught for you!

SANGA-TITI (sitting down again): Now, listen very carefully! While the trader was paying you the money for your ten sacks of cocoa, he deliberately gave you a magic bank-note together with the other one thousand franc notes . . .

ATANGANA (bewildered): a magic bank-note?

(The others listen carefully.)

SANGA-TITI: A magic bank-note! It had the following distinction: if it was

Act Four

kept together with ordinary bank notes, it would attract all the others during the night, and take them back to the trader to whom you had sold your cocoa!

ALL: Hee yeeaah!

SANGA-TITI: Didn't you see a large flock of birds going towards Sangmélima one day?

ALL: We saw the birds! The witch-doctor speaks the truth! . . . We saw the birds!

SANGA-TITI (modestly): My fetishes never tell lies!

ATANGANA: What should I do then, witch-doctor?

SANGA-TITI: Just listen to me again! As you couldn't have known about the magic note without the help of a powerful witch-doctor like me, you unfortunately kept it together with the money you received as a bride-price for your daughter. And so, all your money was taken to Sang-mélima two days ago!

ATANGANA (staring): But I received the bride-price this very afternoon!

SANGA-TITI (to his ASSISTANT): Let's go! This man doesn't want us to find out who stole his money!

ANTANGANA (in despair): Oh . . . don't go, witch doctor! I'll have yet another ram caught for you! Yes, sit down! I'm only an ignorant old man! Ah Ondua! You'll give me your old ram!

(ONDUA is heard muttering something rather unkind about the sort of people who keep borrowing rams from others, and how he was looking forward to eating his own ram on Independence Day, etc. But ATANGANA carries on.)

ATANGANA: Yes, you'll give me your old ram! I'll buy you another one when I go to Sangmé . . .

(Suddenly recollecting.)

Yeeaah! These magicians of Sangmélima! I'll never sell my cocoa there again! . . . I'll be selling only in Zoetele! Do carry on, witch-doctor!

SANGA-TITI (who had sat down as early as when another ram was mentioned): Well, as I was saying, the magic bank-note took all your money to Mount Koupe.

KOUMA (from behind the crowd): Haven't you just said the money was taken to Sangmélima?

SANGA—TITI (offended by this remark by a layman): Who dares to contradict me there? Is there anybody in this village who doesn't know that Mount Koupe is somewhere near Sangmélima?

ALL (trying to stop KOUMA who is forcing his way to the fire): The witch-doctor speaks the truth!

Three Suitors: One Husband

SANGA-TITI (explaining to his supporters): The big city Ngabindele is also on that mountain. That's where magicians make and sell lots of powerful fetishes!

KOUMA (now closer to the fire): Is Ngaoundere so close to Sangmélima?

SANGA-TITI (scornfully): So you didn't know that? What did they teach you at school?

KOUMA (pointing to one direction with one hand): Ngaoundere is in the North!

(Pointing to the opposite direction with the other hand.)

And Sangmélima is in the South!

SANGA-TITI (speaking with doctoral authority, he too points to one direction with one hand): What is the North?

(Pointing to the other direction with the other hand.)

And what's the South?

(The joining both hands above his head.)

Isn't it the same thing?

KOUMA (laughing): But . . .

MBARGA (impatiently): Ah ka, Kouma! Why are you trying to offend the witch-doctor? I know you young men of today never listen to your elders, but this is no schoolboy's stuff!

KOUMA: Is he going to find the money with these tricks?

MBARGA: And you? Are you going to find the money with your questions?

SANGA-TITI (in an attempt to re-establish his shaking authority): Where's the headman of this village?

(MBARGA clears his throat in dignified answer.)

Now, listen to me! So long as you've got people like that young man in this village, never ask me to come to Mvoutessi again!

ATANGANA (appalled): Ah ka, witch-doctor! Don't pay any attention! It's just what I told you! They're all like that in this village! Nobody wants me to . . .

SANGA-TITI (brandishing his antelope horn): If anyone else here dares to contradict me, I'll bewitch this whole village!

ALL (some rushing back in terror): Eeaa keeaah!

ATANGANA: O witch-doctor! I only want to recover my money!

SANGA-TITI (looking into his antelope horn again): My fetishes say that if you want to recover your money, you'd have to give me fifteen cockerels, twelve goats, two rams, and six pigs. Then I'd conjure up the evil spirits I told you about to change your magic bank-notes into ordinary ones again. After all that, you'd have to take some powerful fetishes to

Act Five

Sangmélima two full moons after the theft. You'd recover your money only after bewitching the trader you sold your cocoa to; but never forget to bewitch all the policemen of Sangmélima as well!

MBARGA (bewildered): What? Bewitch all the policemen of Sangmélima?

SANGA-TITI (as the VILLAGERS are beginning to utter angry exclamations): I tell you again, that's the only way to recover the money!

(The angry whispers become more distinct and threatening.)

MBARGA (furious): And what about all the things we gave you?

SANGA-TITI (he and his ASSISTANT are now prudently moving to the road): Haven't I told you what to do if . . .

ALL (rushing towards the WITCH-DOCTOR and his ASSISTANT): You liar . . . You scoundrel . . . You robber . . . etc.

(They drive both of them out, and there is a quick curtain on the confused scene.)

ACT FIVE

The same place next day — a particularly sunny afternoon. The men of the village are gathered in front of ATANGANA's main house. MBARGA, ABESSOLO and ATANGANA are softly talking, and uttering loud, rather frightened exclamations from time to time. ONDUA and MEZOE are drinking their usual palm wine without much enthusiasm. ABESSOLO is preparing some dry tobacco leaves for his pipe, and chewing cola nuts. It is obvious that they are all resigned to their unhappy fate, and expecting the police to turn up any moment now.

ATANGANA (clapping his hands): Hee yeeaah . . . ! This is death itself, Mbarga! Three hundred thousand francs!

ABESSOLO. A great civil servant who promised to bring me lots of cola nuts!

MBARGA: The police coming!

ABESSOLO (vindictively): And all this because of Juliette, that foolish girl!

MEZOE: She was corrupted by secondary school!

ONDUA (filling up his tumbler): Yes, corrupted by secondary school! You know, a lot of people used to say to me: 'Ah, Ondua! You ought to be

ashamed of yourself! When are you sending Matalina to secondary school
like your brother Atangana's sending Juliette?' And I used to say to
them: 'You don't know what you're talking about! Why don't you just
shut up and drink your palm wine? Me, send a daughter of mine to
secondary school? Never! She'll stay at home and grow peanuts like my
wife Monica! And some day, she'll attract us a wealthy suitor who'll
bring me lots of strong drinks!'

(He begins drinking: the others nod in silent approval.)

MEZOE: You were right, ah Ondua! Girls should never be sent to school!
Take Juliette, for instance: what did she do when we told her to love the
civil servant? Did she even listen to us?

ALL: Not at all!

MEZOE: You know what they taught her at Dibamba? They taught her to
disobey her family!

ATANGANA (shaking his head): And speak when *I* am speaking!

ABESSOLO: Didn't I warn you? Didn't this whole village hear me say to
you again and again: 'Ah Atangana, my son! Don't waste all your money
on a girl! Girls are nothing! Build yourself a large house, or get your son
a wife!' But you wouldn't listen to me! You say I'm an old fool! And
now . . .

ATANGANA (annoyed): I've already told you that . . .

MBARGA (getting up): Don't start arguing again like a crowd of women!
Listen to me!

ABESSOLO (almost mechanically): Speak, ah Mbarga!

MBARGA: Where is Oyônô?

ATANGANA: I sent him to Melomebae this morning to see Ntsama, our
nephew. You know he's just been paid a large sum of money for one of
his younger sisters . . .

MEZOE: That was very wise of you! Ntsama wouldn't let us down! His
mother was born here! He would *never* let us down!

ONDUA: Never! Besides his wife Maria is related to the civil servant Mbia:
they both belong to the tribe Esse!

MBARGA: Good, good, but we must also try something else! Ah Atangana!
You must take Juliette to Yaoundé: a girl like her will certainly attract
other suitors in the city! Call at all Government offices, and try to get
rid of your daughter! If someone agrees to pay you three hundred
thousand francs, you give him Juliette right away!

MEZOE (surprised): And where's he going to find such a wealthy man?

MBARGA: Don't you worry, Mezôé! Where do you think all the great
men are?

(Confidentially.)

Act Five

Besides, if you have an attractive daughter, you can do anything these days!

(Angry female voices are heard in the kitchen. JULIETTE is apparently having an argument with the other women.)

ONDUA: I think you must do as Mbarga says, Atangana! You must go and find us a great man!

(Louder.)

Ah Juliette! . . . Juliette!

(But JULIETTE was coming out of the kitchen. She comes up to ATANGANA and looks at him questioningly.)

ATANGANA: Get ready, Juliette! We'll soon be leaving for Yaoundé! We must find you a husband!

JULIETTE (taken aback): Another one? Just how many husbands are you giving me?

MBARGA (explaining what to him looks like a perfectly normal situation): You know we must find somebody wealthy enough to pay back your first suitors!

(BELLA, who was following JULIETTE, had been listening to MBARGA, and nodding in silent approval.)

JULIETTE: And where do you expect to find such a man?

BELLA (moving towards JULIETTE): In the city, my child! They're going to find you a wealthy white man in the city!

JULIETTE (sarcastically): Where in the city? In the market place?

ABESSOLO (offended): How dare you joke in such a situation? Don't you realise all that is involved?

JULIETTE (quickly): I realise that far better than you think! I'm still for sale as far as you're concerned, and I'm not to be consulted for anything.

(Mysteriously.)

But who knows? Someone may come along, and pay you the whole thing!

ATANGANA (suddenly becoming a sugar-daddy): And if that man comes, will you marry him, my child?

JULIETTE: I'll marry the first man who pays you three hundred thousand francs at once!

ALL: Ya a ah!

JULIETTE (firmly): But you'll have to settle the marriage on the spot, without asking for any terylene suits . . .

MEZOE (disgustedly): Ah ka ka ka!

JULIETTE (same as above): No rams, no pigs . . .

ATANGANA (distressed): Aaa keeaaah!

JULIETTE: And no cola nuts!

(ABESSOLO pretends to leave.)

You'll have nothing else on top of the three hundred thousand francs!
Ask the very first man who comes along and I'll . . .

(Unfortunately for JULIETTE, the trader TCHETGEN comes in just
then, with a bundle of merchandise on his head. He is wearing the
traditional robe and sandals of the Bamileke and Bamoun regions. There
are big smiles around when he appears.)

ATANGANA: Ah! There comes Mr Tchetgen!

(Softly, to the audience.)

And these Bamileke traders have got lots of money, I can tell you that!
Just wait and see!

TCHETGEN (putting down his bundle): Good morning everybody!

ALL (very warmly): Mbolo o o!

TCHETGEN (undoing his bundle): I've brought you cheap, very cheap
things from Mbalmayo! Cheap, very cheap! See for yourself!

(He throws some of his stuff around — very cheap things indeed: old
European suits, coats, dresses, etc. The VILLAGERS examine them for
some time, and try them on. MEZOE tries on an ageless dinner jacket
with scarlet woman trousers. TCHETGEN helps him while exclaiming in
sincere appreciation.)

TCHETGEN: Very smart! Very smart indeed!

(MATALINA and MAKRITA also come out of the kitchen to have a
look at the merchandise. MBARGA nudges ATANGANA to go ahead
and propose the deal.)

ATANGANA (hesitantly): Mr Tchetgen, er . . . how many shops have you
got?

TCHETGEN (leaving MEZOE): Oh . . . Two shops in Sangmélima, and a
bar in Zoételé.

ALL: A great man!

(They come closer, looking encouragingly at ATANGANA.)

ABESSOLO (spoiling ATANGANA's tactics): Have you got any cola nuts
from the North in your region?

TCHETGEN (proudly): In the Bamileke region, we've got far better colas
than in the North!

ABESSOLO (excitedly, while the others are trying to stop him): It's him!
It's him, I tell you!

TCHETGEN (surprised): Me?

Act Five

ABESSOLO (to ATANGANA who is resentfully looking at him): What are you waiting for? Here's the great man we need! They've got cola nuts in his region!

JULIETTE (quickly): But . . .

ABESSOLO (sharply): What have you just promised?

(To TCHETGEN, with an engaging smile.)

Mr Tchetgen, you Bamileke traders can be rather miserly!

TCHETGEN (shrugging: he has heard that very often in his career): What do you expect, Mr Abessólô? The Government authorities have been making things very difficult for us lately! For some time now, I've had to pay for everything: licences, fines, fines, licences. Besides, as I haven't been able as yet to meet Medola, the new police commissioner of Zoételé . . .

ATANGANA (anxious to start real business): There, Mr Tchetgen, you see my daughter Juliette? You can marry her! I give her to you!

(Even a keen businessman like TCHETGEN is taken by surprise. However, following an old tradition, he decides to see what he would gain or lose in the bargain. He therefore goes to take a close though rather cautious look at JULIETTE, and he is heard muttering to himself later on.)

TCHETGEN: Not bad! . . . Not bad at all!

(Then louder, to ATANGANA.)

Did you say you want to give her to me?

ATANGANA (smiling): If you like!

JULIETTE (indignantly): I'm not for . . .

MBARGA (thundering): Going to start again? You don't think you've caused us enough trouble already?

JULIETTE: But . . .

ATANGANA (raising his arm in a hardly equivocal way): Shut up!

(JULIETTE runs to MAKRITA in terror. ATANGANA, who is anxious to dispell any doubts TCHETGEN might have conceived because of JULIETTE's uncooperative behaviour, carries on with due paternal pride.)

ATANGANA: You see, Mr Tchetgen? The most obedient girl in the world! You know, some girls today have to be silenced with a stick, and more often that not, even that doesn't work! We're no complicated people here in Mvoutessi when it comes to marriage! You may take Juliette away as soon as you like!

TCHETGEN (coming to the point): How much?

MBARGA: Only three hundred thousand francs!

(He then looks at TCHETGEN in a 'what's that for a great man like you' way.)

TCHETGEN (knocked out): Kooh! So much money just for a woman?

ATANGANA (explaining): You see, I sent her to secondary school, and that's an expensive business, I can tell you that! She speaks French very well . . .

MATALINA: She can also sew . . .

MAKRITA: Make embroiderings . . .

ATANGANA: And cook . . . er . . . sometimes, that is!

ABESSOLO: In brief, she can do anything a white woman can do! Also, as my son was saying, she speaks French . . .

MBARGA: She can also speak English! Interesting, ha, Mr Tchetgen? For your trade!

TCHETGEN: Because she knows so many things, I'll only pay one hundred and fifty thousand francs!

ALL (disapprovingly): Ah ka ka ka!

MBARGA (methodically counting on his fingers): She can also speak English, Espăna, Espănol, Spanish, all these languages they teach at Dibamba!

TCHETGEN (impressed): Kooh! Five languages!

ABESSOLO (not too casually): Not to mention Bulu, of course!

TCHETGEN (matter-of-factly): But what do you expect me to do with all these languages? I only need pidgin English for my trade! However, I think I'll go up to two hundred thousand francs!

(They all grunt in dissatisfaction. That is when OKO and KOUMA come in. OKO is dressed up like a great man, i.e., he is wearing a very elaborate traditional costume, and smoking a longer pipe than ABESSOLO's. KOUMA and OKO are preceded by six MUSICIANS playing 'balafos', or local xylophones. The bewildered VILLAGERS make room for the newcomers. JULIETTE is, of course, more surprised than anybody else. After some time, KOUMA signals to the musicians to stop playing, and he says.)

KOUMA: O my fathers! Let me introduce to you . . .

(Pointing at OKO.)

. . . a very great man!

(A pause.)

Greater than a great civil servant!

ALL (incredulously): Greater than a great civil servant!

KOUMA: Much greater! He studied in the greatest schools in the white men's country, so he's a Doctor of Mathematics!

Act Five

(As there is no noticeable reaction, KOUMA pauses, somewhat disconcerted. Then MBARGA asks.)

MBARGA: He's a what?

KOUMA: A Doctor of Mathematics! That's to say, he can count all the leaves on a palm-tree!

ALL (having understood): Hee yeeaah!

KOUMA: Also, as a Doctor of white languages, he's fluent in French, English, German, Spanish, German, English, French!

ALL: A great man! A great man!

KOUMA: Yes, a great man, but that's not all! Do you know why he came here with such a big escort? He's just been appointed the highest commissioner you can imagine: a High Commissioner!

MBARGA: A what?

KOUMA (raising his hand above his head): A High . . . High commissioner!

MBARGA (imitating KOUMA): Higher than all the commissioners of Sangmélima?

KOUMA: Much higher!

MBARGA (to the others): Then he's the very man we need!

ABESSOLO (excitedly): Yes! And he'll imprison the . . . er . . .

(Lowering his hand to about a yard above the floor.)

. . . er the 'low commissioners' whom the civil servant and Ndi threatened to send here to arrest us!

KOUMA (amused): That's precisely his job! Didn't I tell you he studied in the white men's country? He'll have them imprisoned in accordance with laws that now exist, will exist, or don't exist!

ALL (exulting): Ya a a ah!

KOUMA: You haven't heard everything yet!

(Pompously.)

This great man, this man so great, nay, this grand man . . .

(A pause to prepare his effect.)

. . . well . . . isn't married!

(Exclamations of surprise, and indeed, of hope in the crowd.)

MBARGA (incredulously): What? He's a bachelor? Such a great man?

KOUMA: A bachelor!

(Confidentially.)

And yet, if he only wished to do so, he could marry five women the same day with all the money he earns!

Three Suitors: One Husband

ABESSOLO (moving closer to KOUMA): Then what's he waiting for?

KOUMA: He wants his wife to be as educated as himself!

ALL (spontaneously pointing at JULIETTE): Juliette!

KOUMA (not even looking at JULIETTE): She must have been to secondary school!

MBARGA (quickly taking KOUMA aside): Listen, my son! You know very well that your cousin Juliette would qualify to marry any great man in the world! But . . .

(Discreetly pointing at OKO.)

. . . er . . . do you think he'll be able to find three hundred thousand francs to pay us the bride-price?

KOUMA (softly, to MBARGA): Three hundred thousand francs? Come on! What's that for a High Commissioner? Pocket money!

MBARGA (relieved, to KOUMA): In that case, he'll marry Juliette, and save this whole village!

(Louder, to OKO.)

Mr . . . er . . . white languages . . . er . . .

(Softly, to KOUMA.)

What did we say the great man was?

(As KOUMA is coming to his rescue.)

It's all right! I've got it!

(Louder.)

Mr . . .

(Repeating ABESSOLO's gesture as indicated above.)

Mr Low Commissioner, we've decided to give you our daughter Juliette!

(There is a rather uneasy pause. OKO is calmly smoking his long pipe – incidentally, he has found himself an obvious seat far away from JULIETTE – while the VILLAGERS are anxiously waiting for him to answer. Then, just as MBARGA is clearing his throat again, he says quietly.)

OKO: Well, thank you very much, Sir! What does she think about that?

MBARGA: Who?

OKO: Your daughter!

MBARGA (puzzled): Think? About what?

OKO: About being given to me.

MBARGA (who can't help laughing at the good joke): That's none of her business, Mr Low Commissioner! Besides, what would you expect any sensible girl to think about being given to a very great man? How many girls today wouldn't be happy to marry even a . . . er . . .

Act Five

(With the appropriate gesture.)

A high . . . er . . .

(Correcting himself and his gesture.)

. . . a low commissioner?

(After thankfully nodding at KOUMA who helped him to get the titles right.)

Don't you know that most great men today only prefer to keep many mistresses because they've got lots of girls running after their money?

OKO (waving his pipe to and fro): That's not my point! I quite appreciate the favour you do me. But I would like to hear your daughter herself saying 'yes'!

(The VILLAGERS exchange surprised glances and remarks.)

ATANGANA (the only one to have really understood): I see what's bothering you, my son! My name is Atangana! I'm Juliette's own father! Don't you listen to anyone else here except me!

ONDUA (offended, to the audience): You see what I told you? Atangana's always trying to cut us out of his family!

ATANGANA (to OKO): Juliette is the most obedient daughter in the world! If I say to her:

(Pointing at OKO himself.)

'Love this man' . . .

(Then scornfully pointing at TCHETGEN who is busy making up his bundle up again.)

'Don't love that one there' . . . she only does as I say! No discussion! so don't worry about her! Just give me three hundred thousand francs, and the marriage is settled!

OKO: You still haven't got my point! I'll marry your daughter only if she herself agrees!

MBARGA (rather surprised to see a great man so slow in understanding): Haven't we told you she only does as *we* say?

OKO (quietly): If she's to marry me, she must do as *she* wants!

ABESSOLO (disgustedly, staring at the others): Do as she wants? A woman? Zua Meka!

KOUMA (conciliatingly): Why, this is a simple matter! The great man is quite willing to marry Juliette! He only wants her to say 'yes' to him.

(Softly, to MBARGA.)

Wouldn't it be easier and quicker to ask Juliette to say 'yes' to the great man?

MBARGA (shocked): Ask her to say 'yes'? You mean she would dare to say 'no'?

KOUMA (softly): She's left free to choose, you see!

MBARGA (exasperated by all this nonsense): Ah Kouma! Can't you explain to Mr Dr of palm-tree leaves . . . er . . . Doctor of Spanish and Espanol that women don't speak here in Mvoutessi! We've decided to give him Juliette! What has *she* got to do with it?

KOUMA (pleading): Everything, as a matter of fact, since she's the one who's getting married! Wouldn't it be better for her to choose her own husband?

ABESSOLO (hurt): Why? Because she's a better judge than her whole family?

KOUMA: No: because she's more directly involved.

MBARGA: And we? Where do we come in?

KOUMA: You don't come in. You just wait and see!

ABESSOLO (indignantly): Wait and see! You want her to start that nonsense about marrying her Leclerc schoolboy from Ambam all over again! Never!

KOUMA (smiling): Now that she's seen this great man, I doubt she'll even think of the young man you call her Leclerc schoolboy from Ambam.

(To JULIETTE.)

Well, Juliette, what have you got to say about all this?

JULIETTE (most unconcernedly): All what?

KOUMA: Well . . . all these suitors!

JULIETTE: Which suitors? Please list them. There are so many of them already that I no longer know where I am!

KOUMA (counting with palm-tree leaves, in the old Bulu manner): The first suitor on the list is Ndi, the farmer, who paid one hundred thousand francs for you. A nice young man who wouldn't see any of us here in this village without offering him something to drink! He's also . . .

ALL (impatiently): Ah ka, Kouma! Carry on!

KOUMA (after laying the leaf on the floor, and raising another one): Next, we have the great civil servant Mbia, from Sangmélima, who paid two hundred thousand francs to marry you. He's got a big car, sacks of cola nuts from the North, large Government offices, and of course, a few dozen police commissioners . . .

MBARGA (somewhat frightened): Carry on, my son! Those people may find us here!

KOUMA (now raising a third leaf): The third suitor doesn't really need any formal introduction, being represented by himself, Mr Tchetgen, the trader, who . . .

TCHETGEN (walking off with his bundle of merchandise on his head): I'm not interested! . . . She costs too much!

Act Five

(He is heard muttering as he reaches the road.)

Three hundred thousand francs just for a woman . . . ! Kooh!

KOUMA (looking round): Is that all? Am I forgetting anybody?

MBARGA (surprised): And what about the great man you just brought here?

KOUMA: Oh . . . yes! I nearly forgot! You see, I wanted to make sure he was the only one left on the list!

(He claps his hands.)

Now everybody, here's the last of our suitors, Mr Oko, the man greater than a great civil servant. He studied in the greatest schools in the white men's country, where he was awarded the degree of . . .

(Softly, to MBARGA like one scholar consulting a learned colleague.)

What did we say he was?

MBARGA (confidently): A Doctor of . . . A Doctor of the Doctorate!

KOUMA: Yes, Mr Oko, Doctor of the Doctorate. He's also, as I'm told, a Doctor of the Bachelor . . .

MBARGA (now that he has a chance to display his learning): And a Doctor of palm-tree leaves!

KOUMA: He's also a very wealthy man on top of that, fluent in many white languages and in Spanish:

(With the appropriate gestures.)

High and Low Commissioner . . .

(To JULIETTE.)

How do these titles appeal to you, my cousin?

(A pause. Everybody is anxiously looking at JULIETTE who, since she is the centre of attention, does everything without undue hurry.)

JULIETTE: You want me to take my pick?

KOUMA: Please yourself!

(He points at the four leaves on the floor, and JULIETTE moves closer to them, pretending to look at them thoughtfully. ATANGANA, who cannot afford to let her blunder, timidly points at the leaf representing OKO while addressing the most eloquent winks to his daughter.)

JULIETTE (suddenly making up her mind): I think I'll take the last leaf!

ALL (exulting): Ya a a ah!

ATANGANA (beaming, to OKO): You see? The most obedient daughter in the world!

(Reaching out his hand.)

Where is the bride-price?

OKO (to the leading MUSICIAN): Azele!

Three Suitors: One Husband

MUSICIAN: Massa?

OKO (carelessly): Give the man three hundred thousand francs!

(The leading MUSICIAN gives the money to ATANGANA, who begins counting it with ABESSOLO and MBARGA. Then he plays a jolly theme on his balafo, which is followed up and developed by his companions. Some of the actors present begin dancing. When they have finished, ATANGANA takes JULIETTE by the arm, and pushes her towards OKO.)

ATANGANA: There you are, my son! . . . She's your wife!

(BELLA and the other women utter the 'Oyenga': Ooo-oo-oo-oo-etc.)

ONDUA (scandalised): Ah Atangana! What about the drinks? How can you forget your own brother when you settle Juliette's marriage?

MEZOE: And what about . . .

KOUMA (conciliatingly, as usual): What are you doing, my fathers? Is this how you celebrate the marriage of your daughter? Do you want this great man to get angry like Mbia?

(He takes ONDUA aside and says.)

Don't worry, Tita Ondua! We'll have lots of strong drinks! Why do you think the great man brought his musicians here? He wants us to dance to celebrate his marriage! I tell you again, we'll have lots of strong drinks!

ONDUA (suddenly cheering up): Lots of strong drinks, you say?

KOUMA: Lots of strong drinks! . . . And a dance!

ONDUA (to the others, at the top of his voice): A dance . . . a dance . . .

ALL (beginning to clear the stage): A dance . . . a dance . . . Let's dance!

ATANGANA (while the MUSICIANS are getting ready for the dance): So I've now received the bride-price for my daughter!

(He moves towards JULIETTE who is standing near her new husband.)

You know, my child, I might as well have given you for nothing . . .

(Confidentially to avoid being overheard by OKO.)

To that Leclerc schoolboy of yours, for instance!

(He begins laughing at his own joke, then goes to join the others who are now almost ready for the dance. MBARGA has just had the not unfamiliar armchair brought out again, and set at the usual place for OKO. Then, as MEZOE is foolishly bringing out a much more modest armchair for JULIETTE, the headman, who sees to it that things are done properly in Mvoutessi, quickly signals to him to take the armchair back, and bring a stool instead. When this is done, and JULIETTE is dutifully sitting beside OKO, AZELE, the leading MUSICIAN plays a theme on his instrument, which is followed up and developed as above. MEZOE and ONDUA may help with drum accompaniment. JULIETTE

Act Five

and OKO will join in after a while. Even MBARGA will condescend to dance. The ACTORS will, of course, ask those members of the audience who have stayed through all the foregoing events to take part in the celebrations of JULIETTE's marriage to OKO. The curtain will not go down until everybody is exhausted . . .)

Until Further Notice

For Dr Bernard Fonlon, with love

The radio version of UNTIL FURTHER NOTICE was recorded for the
BBC External Services in April, 1967. The cast included:

ABESSOLO	Lionel Ngakane
CECILIA	Jumoke Debayo
MEZOE	Femi Euba
ADA	Juliana John
MEKA	David Longond
NKATEFOE	Alex Tetteh-Lartey
THE DRIVER	Willie Jonah

Produced by Douglas Cleverdon

The stage version printed here: received its first performance at the
Y.W.C.A. Hall, Randolph Place, Edinburgh in August, 1967. The cast
included the following members of the Drama Group of the University
of Keele:

ABESSOLO	Ray Johnson
CECILIA, his wife	Louise Robinson
MEZOE, his son	John Hartock
ADA, his daughter	Julie Cornelius
TITA-MONGO, his grandson	Tim Harris
MEKA, a relative	Dave Radstone
NKATEFOE, the preacher	Mac Elsey
A DRIVER	Tim Fletcher
HIS COMPANION	
TWO OTHER CHILDREN, Abessôlô's grandsons	

Produced by Tim Fletcher

We are in Mvoutessi, a little village in the southern part of East Cameroun. This is ABESSOLO's home, and the actors will mainly be sitting inside a temporary palm tree hall 'elum' which has been erected in front of the main house, as is customary in the Bulu region when important visitors are expected. There are lots of local musical instruments about: drums, tom-toms, balafos, etc. and a large number of seats. Also, the presence of several calabashes and demijohns of palm wine at the far corner of the hall suggests that there will be lots of rejoicing when the visitors arrive. A small table is placed somewhere further back, with NKATEFOE's Bible, hymn books and old fashioned glasses. The road is on the left; only the hedge separating it from the village, and the little open space between the palm-tree hall and the hedge, can be seen. CECILIA's kitchen is on the right, although not seen by the audience. The general atmosphere is one of impatient expectation. When the curtain rises, ABESSOLO and his relatives are just finishing a meal. They are sitting in a half circle, and eating out of three or four common bowls placed in front of them.

ABESSOLO (stops eating for a while and points at one of the three little boys): Now . . . look at that one there! Don't fill your spoon like that, you greedy little thing! A true man never fills his spoon like a lorry!

(Scornfully, looking at the children in turn.)

He e e! They're all strong men now, because it's time to eat, and not to go and fetch some water for their old grandmother! They dread water! One would think the little brook behind our house is full of crocodiles! Eating is the only job Tita-Mongô and his brothers are anxious to learn! Nobody will ever expect you anywhere like we're expecting your aunt Matalina and my son-in-law this afternoon!

NKATEFOE (moving back to the little table): Who knows, Abessôlô? Don't you see how little children of yesterday become great people overnight? Who would have thought, only four years ago when our daughter Matalina was going to France, that she'd find herself such a great husband?

(He shakes his head wisely.)

Things change quickly today!

MEKA (who is still eating, and desperately trying to swallow a reluctant mouthful of food): They do! They do! Our fathers used to say: 'Girls are nothing'. And yet, Mata . . . lina . . . Mat . . . Mat . . .

(He chokes himself and begins coughing while reaching for the calabash of water placed near TITA-MONGO.)

ABESSOLO (quickly): Pass him the calabash of water!

Until Further Notice

(TITA-MONGO is slow to obey.)

Doesn't Tita-Mongô hear what I say?

TITA-MONGO (shaking the calabash): It's almost empty! Grandmother didn't bring any . . .

ABESSOLO (scandalised): Zua Meka! No water?

(Shouting.)

Ah . . . Cécilia! Cécilia!

(All they hear is CECILIA and some other WOMEN laughing loudly in the kitchen.)

NKATEFOE: I don't think anybody will hear you there!

ABESSOLO: They won't! Cécilia and the other women of this village always laugh like unmarried women! You, Tita-Mongô! Run and ask your grandmother whether we should be eating like birds!

(TITA-MONGO runs out. To MEKA who is still coughing.)

Take it easy, Meka! The water will be here in a moment!

(To the two other children who were busy finishing their meal.)

And you! You've eaten quite enough already!

(One LITTLE BOY suddenly begins licking a plate.)

Don't lick the plate with your tongue, or you'll never have any luck with women in later life!

(Shaking a threatening fly-whisk at them.)

Go to the kitchen, all of you!

(In a softened voice, as the CHILDREN go out.)

Go and help your mother Ada get things ready for your little aunt Matalina and her hus . . .

CECILIA (off stage): Start peeling the plantains, Ada! I'll soon . . .

ABESSOLO (aggressively, as CECILIA comes in): There she is at last with the water! Must I lose my voice calling you?

CECILIA: Don't you hear all that noise in the kitchen?

(She gives a bowl of water to MEKA who starts drinking.)

ABESSOLO: A married woman always tells her visitors: 'Don't laugh so loudly! My ears are where my husband is!'

(To MEKA who is still drinking.)

Yes . . . drink, Meka! These women will certainly kill somebody in this village with their foolishness. To bring us such a hot dish, and no water to wash it down! I keep telling them about Azegue Eba who died like that in . . .

CECILIA (impatiently): Meka's all right now.

Until Further Notice

MEKA (softly clearing his throat): Ha a ah! . . . ha a a ah!

NKATEFOE: Drink some more water!

(MEKA drinks some more water.)

There! . . . Would be a pity to die from Cécilia's excellent food!

(CECILIA smiles at the compliment.)

MEKA (speaking with difficulty): I've . . . I've swallowed it! . . . Haa ah!

(He returns the bowl to CECILIA.)

CECILIA (good-humouredly): Meka never leaves his witchcraft behind!

ABESSOLO: It's all your fault! You . . .

CECILIA: We've got a lot to do in the kitchen! You know that Matalina and her husband are coming!

MEKA (as though he wanted to test his voice): Coming soon, aren't they?

CECILIA: Abessôlô's the one who knows the exact time. I was away when they brought him the letter.

ABESSOLO: Didn't Mezôé read the letter to us again and again?

(To MEKA.)

You'd better wait for Mezóé himself. I sent him to Zoétéle this morning to catch a ram, but he should be back soon. He's the only one in this village who's actually seen our son-in-law. He went to Yaoundé four weeks ago to visit them.

NKATEFOE (putting on his glasses): Three full moons they've been back from France . . .

ABESSOLO: Three full moons! And Matalina has never said to her husband: 'Let's go and visit my fathers and mothers in Mvoutessi, the little village where I was born . . . '

(Resentfully looking at CECILIA.)

I've always said that girls . . .

CECILIA (quickly): But she wrote!

(To the others.)

She wrote that she and her husband are still waiting for a hospital!

ABESSOLO (scornfully): A hospital! Listen to what she's saying! Have you already forgotten what Mezôé told us?

MEKA (in his normal voice): Mezôé? What did Mezôé tell you?

ABESSOLO (as the noise of an approaching moped is heard): There comes Mezôé himself! He'll be able to tell us all about that!

NKATEFOE (as the motorcyclist slows down): These young people and their things! They can go faster than you would throw a pebble!

Until Further Notice

MEKA (approvingly): Much faster! . . . Yes, they go much faster!

(To ABESSOLO.)

Did Mezôé bring his machine from Yaoundé?

ABESSOLO (while MEZOE is heard parking his moped near the main house): From Yaoundé! His sister had just bought it, and he said to her 'A great woman like you should no longer be using this sort of thing! This is for poor villagers like me! Tell your husband to buy you a big car!'

(A pause: one feels that he is proud of his son's wisdom.)

And he came home with the motorcycle!

MEKA: What else! That's what a man should do!

MEZOE (he raises his hands as he comes from the road): I greet my fathers!

ALL THE MEN: Mbôlô ô ô!

MEZOE: Is everything ready, Na' Cécilia?

CECILIA (picking up the empty bowls): Almost ready. Your sister Ada's just peeling the plantains.

MEZOE (scandalised): The plantains? You mean you're cooking plantains for the doctor?

CECILIA (surprised): Are plantains taboo to him?

MEZOE (who is stating a simple fact): Great people don't eat plantains.

ABESSOLO (uneasily): Didn't I s . . .

CECILIA (sharply): You never said anything!

(To MEZOE.)

Now tell me, Mezôé: what do great people eat?

MEZOE (looking for a seat): Great things, of course. They eat civilised food.

CECILIA (picking up the empty calabash): What's that?

ABESSOLO (impatiently): Let him explain! After all, he's the only one here who's been to the big city! He spent two weeks in his sister's house!

MEZOE (sitting down): I'll explain it to you, ah Na'Cécilia! But . . .

(With a surprised glance at the empty bowls she was taking away.)

. . . er . . . didn't you expect me to come back this afternoon from Zoételé?

ABESSOLO (shouting): Ah Ada! . . . Doesn't Ada hear my voice?

ADA (offstage): Tita a ah!

ABESSOLO: Your brother's back!

NKATEFOE (to MEZOE): Our ears are getting cold!

MEZOE: Be patient!

(CECILIA goes and sits next to ABESSOLO.)

Until Further Notice

You see, whenever people ask me: 'What is it like in your sister's home in Yaoundé?' I ask myself: 'How could I possibly describe all I saw?' Nothing there is like anything here. Believe me, o my fathers, your daughter Matalina did marry a great man!

ALL (proudly): A great man!

MEZOE: My sister never goes shopping like other women, with a basket: she only goes to the big foodstores, where they sell civilised food from the white men's country.

CECILIA: And why does she go there?

MEZOE: Why? Well, because it's more expensive! She must also find vitamins.

CECILIA: Find who?

MEZOE: Vitamins! You only find them in food kept in refrige . . . er . . . you know, these cold, very cold cupboards.

MEKA: And what are these vit . . . these things?

MEZOE (embarrassed): Well . . . what can I say, Tita Meka? You wouldn't understand! Besides, come to mention it, Matalina said I wouldn't understand either!

MEKA (puzzled): But what do they taste like?

(They all laugh.)

ADA (coming in with her brother's food): There you are, Mezôé!

MEZOE (taking the plate): Thank you, Ada! . . . Hmm! . . . The good smell of Na'Cécilia's food!

(He begins eating.)

ABESSOLO (playfully): Be careful, Mezôé! We very nearly mourned Meka just before you came!

(They all laugh again.)

NKATEFOE (to MEZOE, when the laughing has ceased): Our ears are with you, my son!

MEZOE: Well, as I was saying, you don't eat with your hands in Matalina's house. You sit in front of many white little pieces of cloth. I even remember counting as many as seven forks before me . . .

ALL (amazed): What are you saying!

MEZOE: Seven! Big ones, medium-sized ones, small ones.

ABESSOLO: Ah Ada! Where are the seven . . . er . . . the forks of this house? Why don't you go and . . .

MEZOE (as ADA was going to the main house): Never mind, never mind, Tit'Abessôlô! We're in the bush! I'll manage with my hands!

(He begins heartily tearing a leg of chicken.)

Until Further Notice

MEKA (approvingly): What else! That's how we used to eat when we were your age! And we're your fathers, aren't we?

NKATEFOE (somewhat patronising): Things have changed, Meka! The pastor himself was saying so the other day in Ngôlebang! He observed that young people today no longer attend the early morning prayers . . .

CECILIA: They all sleep like antelopes caught in the devil's net! I always tell the parable of the five foolish . . .

ABESSOLO (impatiently): Why don't you shut up, you foolish old woman? Did we gather here to listen to you? Carry on Mezôé!

MEZOE (with his mouth full): You sit in front of your plate, and the majordomo . . .

CECILIA: The what?

MEZOE: The majordomo: the man in charge of their food.

CECILIA (shocked): You mean my daughter doesn't cook for her husband?

MEZOE: You can't expect a girl who's studied in Europe to cook! Africa must change!

CECILIA: Who?

MEZOE: Africa.

CECILIA: And who's that?

MEZOE: Well . . . nobody in particular . . . it's you, and . . .

CECILIA (indignantly): *I am* somebody! Your own mother!

ABESSOLO: Why don't you . . .

CECILIA (same as above): Nobody has ever called me nobody!

MEZOE (appalled): I was only . . .

CECILIA (now thinking back): I was the first girl the generation of your fathers ever married in Mvoutessi, Mezôé!

MEZOE (trying to plead): I was only . . .

CECILIA: Whenever . . .

ABESSOLO (shouting): Why don't you listen to Mezôé? He was going to tell us about Africa!

NKATEFOE: Yes, my son! You were going to tell your fathers about Africa!

(Helpfully, as MEZOE is looking a bit lost.)

You said Africa's nobody . . .

MEZOE (no longer knowing how to express himself): Er . . . that's not exactly what I was trying to say . . .

(Brightening up.)

You see, our village, our tribe, our whole country could all be put down on a map.

MEKA (puzzled again): A what?

MEZOE (going to borrow a sheet of paper from NKATEFOE's notes): A map!

(Sketching a rough map of Africa.)

A drawing on a sheet of paper.

(He comes back to give the drawing to his father.)

That's Africa!

ABESSOLO (triumphantly showing the map to CECILIA): You see, Cecilia? I knew my son Mezoe wouldn't call his own mother 'Africa'!

(CECILIA grunts in satisfaction. ABESSOLO carries on, to show that he has understood.)

And so, my son, we have no more villages, no more tribes, no more countries, only a sheet of paper . . .

MEZOE: A sheet of paper!

ALL: Hee yeea aah!

ADA (getting up): Ah Na'Cécilia!

CECILIA: Yes?

ADA: Let's go and take care of the plantains . . .

MEKA (to ADA who was going to the kitchen): Just a minute, my daughter! Er . . . no need for you to stay, Cécilia!

CECILIA (going to the kitchen): Don't be long, Ada! You know I haven't got the strength to pound plantains . . . My poor arms . . .

MEKA (comfortingly): We're all getting old, Cécilia! We're no longer what we used to be!

(To ADA, when CECILIA is gone.)

Are you and your husband living in peace in Sangmélima?

ADA: Living in peace? Not at all, Tita Meka! He keeps beating me these days . . .

MEKA (incredulously): Beating you? The civil servant? How could . . .

ADA: Beating me, Tita Meka! They've changed a lot in Sangmélima! All of them! This has been going on ever since a Training College for girls was opened there. Our husbands want to get rid of us. They say we have no education, and we can't earn any salaries . . .

(Bitterly.)

Only the girls in the Training College are women now.

ABESSOLO (indignantly): And that man keeps beating her! Beating my daughter! That's why I sent somebody to Sangmélima to tell Ada: 'Your father says: run away! Go back to your village, and take your children with you! Just because your husband paid a few thousand francs to your family doesn't mean he should treat you like a beggar's daughter!'

(The others grunt in approval.)

Your younger sister Matalina has just come back from overseas with her great man! They could easily pay back your husband!

(Threateningly.)

They could even throw him in jail if he doesn't watch out!

MEKA (with a big smile): That was wisely spoken!

NKATEFOE (glancing towards the road): They'll soon be here . . .

MEKA: Any moment now.

(To ADA who is collecting MEZOE's empty plate.)

Yes go and join your mother in the kitchen, Ada. We'll all be saved!

(ADA goes to the kitchen.)

ABESSOLO (to MEZOE): Get your fathers something to drink, my son!

(MEZOE goes to fetch a calabash of palm-wine at the far corner.)

NKATEFOE: Ah Mezôé, what exactly is our son-in-law's job?

MEZOE (confidentially, bringing a calabash of palm-wine): Matalina says he's very likely to be appointed Secretary of State. But . . . .

(Filling up a tumbler for ABESSOLO.)

. . . er . . . I understand he might turn that offer down.

MEKA: Turn it down? But why?

MEZOE (taking the tumbler to his FATHER): I said to him: 'They want to appoint you Secretary of State. Other Doctors of Medicine haven't been so lucky . . . '

NKATEFOE: Hospitals are full of them!

ABESSOLO (trying to get the title correctly): Setrec . . . Secrec . . .

MEZOE (now filling up another tumbler for MEKA): Secretary of State.

MEKA: Is that the man who rules everybody in the city?

MEZOE (giving him the wine): Precisely!

CECILIA (coming in with a basketful of peanuts): Who's that who rules everybody in the city?

MEZOE: The Secretary of State, Mother.

CECILIA (unconcernedly, sitting down): Oh! . . .

(She begins cracking her peanuts.)

MEKA (after a sip of his wine): Then why won't our son-in-law take the job?

MEZOE (filling another tumbler): He says he's always wanted to work in

---

Until Further Notice

one of these little places far away in the bush! Somewhere with lots of patients, and no doctor, where he could really help.

(Then, like an unforgivable sinner, he goes on to offer the tumbler of wine to the PREACHER who, of course, righteously ignores him.)

MEKA (while MEZOE is going back to his seat): *Help?* Our son-in-law wants to *help?*

CECILIA: He does! He told me so in a letter soon after the marriage in the white men's country.

(Proudly.)

Matalina also went there to become a doctor, you know!

MEZOE (sitting down): A midwife.

CECILIA: What's the difference?

ABESSOLO: A doctor is a man; a midwife is his wife.

MEZOE: And a doctor knows more . . .

ABESSOLO (calmly: he is merely stating an eternal truth): Of course . . . being a man . . .

CECILIA: He said he and Matalina would be working in a hospital . . .

NKATEFOE: Our son Mezôé was just telling us . . .

CECILIA: He's a doctor . . .

ABESSOLO (out of patience): And who says he isn't?

CECILIA: Then why doesn't he work in a hospital?

MEZOE (getting impatient too): He's a Doctor of Medicine, that's why!

CECILIA (who is getting a bit confused): You just said that doctors . . .

ABESSOLO (at the top of his voice): Things have changed!

CECILIA: And . . .

ABESSOLO (same as above): We want him to be a great man; not a doctor!

CECILIA (stubbornly): And what's a great man?

ABESSOLO: A Secrec . . . A . . .

MEZOE: A Secretary of State!

MEKA: The man who rules everybody!

ABESSOLO (thoughtfully, getting up): He must take that job!

(To the audience.)

All my brothers and relatives of the tribe Fong once came to me and asked: 'Ah Abessôlô! We hear that our daughter Matalina has just got married overseas to a young man from a far away tribe, in Kribi. We've never seen him. We've received no bride-price; we've eaten no fat oxen; we've had nothing! What does that mean? Are you trying to be the only

Until Further Notice

one to enjoy the benfits of the education we all contributed to give our daughter Matalina?'

(A pause; he carries on more confidentially.)

And I replied to my brothers and relatives: 'Why don't we just wait and see! One no longer asks for the bride-price before marriage nowadays! Let's wait until everything has been done!'

(With a cunning smile.)

We shall then demand money, cattle, anything we like, without anybody saying to us: 'You've already been paid the bride-price for your daughter!'

ALL THE MEN: That was wisely spoken!

ABESSOLO (to the others in the hall): Now, if our son-in-law goes to work in a small hospital in the bush, how is he going to get the money to give us all that we propose to ask him in exchange for our daughter?

ALL THE MEN: How indeed!

MEKA: And what an obedient child Matalina was! She never went back to school without coming to see us the day before, and saying to me: 'Ah Tita Meka! I'll be going back to Metet tomorrow morning!'

CECILIA (with maternal pride): Just like her! Never forgot any of her fathers!

MEKA: Never!

(He pauses to take an expert sip of palm-wine.)

And I always said to her: 'Go to the kitchen, my daughter! Ask your mother Makrita to give you one kilogramme of cocoa. You'll sell it on your way to Metet, in Awae.' As I was saying to Makrita herself the other day, our kilogrammes of cocoa weren't given in vain! The day will soon come when we enjoy the benefits of our love for our daughter Matalina!

NKATEFOE: The wisest daughter we ever begot in this village! Whenever I was sending reports on her behaviour during the long vacations to her school in Metet, I always wrote a special note to the pastor, saying: 'She never attends traditional dances! She never misses a religious service! Above all, she never even speaks to a boy!'

CECILIA: I've always known how to bring up my children!

ABESSOLO (sarcastically): And what about Théresia? What about that daughter of yours who followed her sister to Yaoundé? She was very well brought up, I suppose?

MEZOE (slightly annoyed): Matalina is looking after Théresia! I told you so last week!

ABESSOLO (sceptically): Two whole months she's been gone now . . .

MEZOE: One doesn't master typewriting and shorthand overnight! But Théresia learns very fast indeed: Sheramy's already offering her a job!

Until Further Notice

CECILIA: Who?

MEZOE: Sheramy, the leader of the Black Beagles Band, the 'B.B.B.', as they're called. He met Théresia at the school where she's learning to type, and he offered her a very good job.

NKATEFOE: As a typist?

MEZOE: No, of course not. As a singer in the band.

ABESSOLO (matter-of-factly): Is he a great man too?

MEZOE: Plenty of money. And I warned my sister Théresia to be careful never again to be seen with anybody else. Who knows? Sheramy might want to marry her. One can never attract too many great men in one's family today . . .

ALL THE MEN (like one man): You speak the truth!

MEZOE: No good-looking girl needs stay in her village and grow peanuts like her mother. All she's got to do is to learn to type

CECILIA: And what if she's like Théresia who never went to school?

MEZOE: That's irrelevant. She only has to be good-looking. Besides, if Matalina's husband agrees to become a great man . . .

CECILIA: What exactly would be his job?

ABESSOLO (getting tired of CECILIA's questioning): Are you getting deaf by any chance? He'd be a great man! Can't you understand that?

CECILIA: Who's talking to you? You're always shouting like an old gorilla!

(Roars of laughter.)

MEZOE: You see, Na' Cécilia, a great man only goes to work when he likes . . .

MEKA (proudly): Not like that white man at the saw-mill who always has to get up early to go to work . . .

MEZOE: No, because, in a sense, my brother-in-law would be a whiter man . . .

ALL THE MEN (delightedly): What else!

MEZOE: When he does go to his office, which would, of course be air-conditioned . . .

CECILIA (startled): Air . . . condi . . . what? My son-in-law?

ABESSOLO (exasperated): Is there anything more infuriating than an old woman! Your son is about to reach the top of the tree, and you say to him: 'Come down, so as to start climbing up again!' Can't you listen?

MEZOE (trying to find the right words to use): Air-conditioned, that's to say, he wouldn't be breathing the same air ignorant people like us breathe in the streets. His air would be coming out of a . . . a sort of box . . .

ALL (almost incredulously): A a a aah kee ea ah!

NKATEFOE: And how would he be working?

MEZOE: He wouldn't even have to work! He'd just tell his deputy to tell his porter to tell the people queuing in front of his office to come again, same time, same day, next week . . .

MEKA: And he'd find similar jobs for all his wife's relatives . . .

MEZOE: Yes, he would! After all, what has he given us already in exchange for . . .

ABESSOLO: I tell you again, just be patient! We'll . . .

MEKA (impatiently): Patient? You want us to be patient! Don't you realise that man will soon be getting both his own and the salary of the daughter whose education *we* paid for? Why do you think he wants to take her to that hospital somewhere in the bush? He wants to stop us . . .

ABESSOLO (jumping up): I'm not dead yet! Matalina's salary belongs to us! Our son-in-law will pay the bride-price, but Matalina herself will pay us back the money we spent for her studies!

ALL THE MEN (loudly): Ya a a ah!

MEZOE: I said to Matalina when I was in Yaoundé: 'O my own sister! You know I've got no academic qualifications! I can neither speak nor write French properly. Will you let your brother die as a farmer in Mvoutessi just because he can't pass any examinations? A man with your husband's education has no place among naked people in the bush! My sister, make him change his mind! Make him work in the big city where he could find me a good job!

MEKA (eagerly): And what did Matalina say?

MEZOE: What else could she say? She promised to take my advice . . .

ALL (delightedly): Ya a ah!

MEZOE: She promised! Besides, she wants to work in a big, modern hospital like the one in Yaoundé, where she would only give orders to the less educated girls . . .

MEKA (with conviction): She'll make her husband change her mind.

MEZOE: She will! These girls who have studied in Europe don't usually get married, but when they do, they know how to dominate their husbands. They're emancipated.

CECILIA: They're what?

MEZOE: Emancipated! Like white women. Don't you know Matalina came back with white woman's hair on her head?

CECILIA (utterly shocked): What?

MEZOE: White woman's hair! Didn't I tell you?

ABESSOLO (trying to stop CECILIA speaking): Your sister will find you a good job in the big city, my son.

MEZOE: She will! I also said to her: 'O my sister! You know that all these girls of today only want highly educated husbands. They scorn us, the villagers.'

CECILIA: I've always advised you to find yourself a bush girl, Mezôé.

MEZOE (disillusioned sneer): Don't you know, Na'Cécilia? They too only want great men! They no longer want to grow peanuts and cook casava . . .

CECILIA (with dignity): Girls in my day used to be proud of that!

ABESSOLO (mockingly): Because *yours* was an uncivilised day!

CECILIA (hurt): And what about *your* day? Don't we belong to the same generation?

ABESSOLO: Yes, but I'm not like you!

(With an air of superiority.)

I know things!

CECILIA: When did you go overseas?

ABESSOLO: I sailed to Santa Isabel . . .

CECILIA: That was thirty years ago!

ABESSOLO: But I've crossed the sea! I'm not like you! You never go anywhere! You're just like an egg!

(The others burst out laughing.)

CECILIA (scornfully looking at ABESSOLO): He e e! He went to the Spanish land and he calls it travelling!

ABESSOLO: I've crossed the sea!

CECILIA: Then why didn't they make you a great man?

ABESSOLO: That was before Independence!

CECILIA: And what did you bring back?

ABESSOLO: Lots of things!

CECILIA (her turn to be sarcastic): Yes, lots of things! You also brought a stupid girl who's now cooking for you in the kitchen!

ABESSOLO (accusingly): You frightened her away! You and the other women in this village! Always threatening to beat her up in the bush!

(More laughter.)

CECILIA: Should have stayed and faced us like a real woman! But she couldn't! She couldn't because she was just a little frog!

ABESSOLO (same as above): You wouldn't let me have other wives!

(Resentfully looking at both CECILIA and NKATEFOE.)

You and your missionaries! You say God doesn't like women!

Until Further Notice

MEKA: He doesn't!

(Malciously glancing at NKATEFOE.)

Ask any good priest!

(He bursts out laughing; ABESSOLO and MEZOE join him.)

NKATEFOE (cautiously: theology is not his strong point): Er . . . I think you're mistaking the Catholic God for the true God of the Protestant faith. Our God doesn't dislike women: He only doesn't like it when there are too many of them around . . .

ABESSOLO: I don't blame him! Whoever could stand the wrangling of a crowd of women! Look at Mbarga, the Chief, who's now become as skinny as an orphaned little monkey!

(Big laughter from the men: they are all familiar with the case.)

MEKA: He wouldn't listen to me! I warned him before he left for Akônôlinga! I said to him: 'Ah Mbarga! Be sure not to spend more than one week there with your seventh wife only, while all the others are here, waiting for their own rights!'

ABESSOLO (still laughing): And he spent six whole weeks in Akônôlinga! Six whole weeks! Now he can't get any sleep ever since he's been back!

(The OTHER MEN join in the laughter.)

CECILIA (righteously offended, looking at her husband): Look at him! You'd never hear Abessôlô telling a holy joke! His old pagan eyes always light up when he hears the word 'woman'!

MEKA (playfully): Why do you say that, Cécilia? Have you forgotten what people used to say about the men of our tribe? 'A true Fông may grow white hair on his head, but never on his heart . . . '

ADA (off stage): A na o o oh!

CECILIA: O o o oh!

ADA: Have you finished cracking the peanuts?

CECILIA: I'll bring them!

(She goes to the kitchen with obvious relief: she does not like palm-wine orgies.)

MEZOE (pouring some more wine for his FATHER): One would die laughing listening to my father and his old wife!

(He goes back to his seat.)

I never knew you once had another wife, Tit'Abessôlô!

ABESSOLO (with a faint smile): That was before you were born, my son.

MEKA: A really beautiful girl.

(Like an authority on women.)

As dark as ebony, and fleshy . . . yes, fleshy! Not like the wasps who buzz

Until Further Notice

around you young men today!

ABESSOLO (nostalgically): A woman! Her father was a great Chief in the Spanish land, and he liked me very mcuh. So, when I was leaving, he merely said to his daughter: 'Follow this man!'

(Slowly nodding.)

Eaah! . . . A good land!

(A pause.)

And she was a real woman.

MEKA (enthused): A real woman! We all, the younger men of the village then . . .

(With the usual malicious glance at NKATEFOE.)

. . . even Nkatefoe who's now become a man of God . . . we all used to go and hide in the thickets, near the pool, on the way to the plantations, to see her bathing!

(Big laughter.)

NKATEFOE (with surprising sensuality): Hmm! . . . She was a woman!

ABESSOLO: A woman! And what a good land too! That's where women never speak when men are speaking, and you can cut your wife's head off if she dares to turn her back on you in bed during the night . . . No missionaries, no . . .

NKATEFOE: I'm told things have changed there as well . . .

ABESSOLO (sincerely): A pity . . . a great pity . . .

(A car is heard slowing down.)

Maybe it's them!

MEZOE (jumping up): No, it can't be!

(He runs to the hedge.)

That car isn't a Mercedes.

MEKA (following him): A what?

MEZOE: A Mercedes. The big car all great people travel in.

(He points to the road.)

The car you see stopping there is a 'Deux-Chevaux'.

MEKA: A what?

MEZOE: A 'Deux Chevaux'. That's the French for 'Two Horses'.

MEKA (puzzled as usual): Two horses? They look more to me like two men wearing white uniforms!

MEZOE: It's not the men I mean! It's the car, the car!

MEKA: The car?

Until Further Notice

(Excitedly.)

You mean our son-in-law has sent us this car as part of the bride-price?

ABESSOLO (offended): This isn't the type of car I would accept in exchange for a daughter like Matalina!

(Scornfully.)

Besides it isn't even a car; it's a grasshopper!

NKATEFOE (impatiently): Why don't you wait until the visitors themselves tell us what they came for? They're approaching!

(They all remain standing in the little open space between the palm-tree hall and the hedge. The DRIVER and his COMPANION enter, and raise their hands as they greet them.)

THE DRIVER and HIS COMPANION: We greet you all!

ALL: Mbôlô ô ô!

THE DRIVER: We came to see Abessòlô . . .

ABESSOLO (stepping forward): Here I am myself!

(Proudly.)

The father of my daughter Matalina!

THE DRIVER: We're bringing you a letter and many other things.

ABESSOLO: From the city?

THE DRIVER (approving): From where else!

(He gives ABESSOLO a sealed envelope.)

ABESSOLO (in a worried voice): Isn't Mat . . . isn't my son-in-law coming?

THE DRIVER'S COMPANION: He can't come! With his official duties . . .

MEZOE (eagerly): Did he take the job?

THE DRIVER: Yes, he did; yesterday!

MEZOE (not daring to believe his ears): Secretary of State?

THE DRIVER'S COMPANION: What else!

MEZOE (jumping excitedly): She did it! I knew she would do it!

MEKA: Who? Did what? Tell us, my son!

MEZOE (dancing with joy now): Matalina! Her husband took the job!

ABESSOLO (delighted, embracing his SON): What are you telling me?

MEZOE: Just what I am telling!

(Then, rushing to the drums, he begins beating an enthusiastic rhythm. ABESSOLO, MEKA, and even NKATEFOE, begin dancing, swaying to and fro, under the amused eyes of the DRIVER and his COMPANION. CECILIA and ADA, who have been attracted by the noise, come out. They are thunderstruck at seeing the preacher dance like any normal

Until Further Notice

pagan. MEZOE stops drumming for a while, and NKATEFOE says:)

NKATEFOE: Ah Cécilia, Cécilia! Why don't you dance . . .

(CECILIA stares at him in horror.)

. . . er . . . yes, why don't you dance a holy dance now? Your daughter has done it!

CECILIA (rushing forward): Is she coming?

ABESSOLO (cheerfully): She can't come! Official drinks in the city! Our son-in-law has been appointed a great man!

CECILIA (hopefully): A doctor?

ABESSOLO: A great man! Not a doctor!

CECILIA (speaking to herself): He said he wanted to work in a hospital . . .

THE DRIVER: He's changed his mind.

MEZOE (triumphantly): What did I tell you? Africa must change!

ABESSOLO (waving the envelope): And he sent me a letter! A letter from his own hand! . . . To me!

(He gives the letter to MEZOE.)

You read us the letter, my son!

(MEZOE begins tearing the envelope while the DRIVER and his COMPANION return to the road to unload the car. They will be bringing cases of wine, beer, etc. while the following goes on.)

MEZOE (emphatically, like a new Prefect making an important speech): République Fédérale du Cameroun . . . '

CECILIA: That's not my son-in-law!

ABESSOLO: Why don't you shut up! We want to listen to the letter!

MEZOE (same as above): 'Son Excellence Monsieur le Secrétaire d'Etat . . .'

MEKA: What are you doing, my son? Have you forgotten that your fathers don't understand French?

MEZOE (translating): 'His Excellency the Secretary of State regrets to inform you that due to unforseen events . . . '

CECILIA (who had moved closer to MEZOE): This is *not* my son-in-law's handwriting!

MEZOE (impatiently): Of course it isn't!

(Displaying the lteter.)

The letter is typewritten!

CECILIA: What?

MEZOE (pointing at the lines): Typewritten! His secretary typed it.

CECILIA (surprised): Didn't you say he is himself . . .

Until Further Notice

MEZOE: A Secretary, yes. But he also has a secretary.

CECILIA: But . . .

ABESSOLO (shouting): Things have changed!

CECILIA: And so . . .

ABESSOLO (proudly): Our son-in-law will now be sitting in a large office . . .

MEKA: Breathing educated air out of a box . . .

ABESSOLO: And telling his deputy to tell the people queuing in front of his office to tell the porter to come again, same time, same day, next week!

MEZOE: Above all, he's going to find similar jobs for all his wife's relatives!

THE DRIVER'S COMPANION (bringing the last case of beer): The car is unloaded, o my father!

ABESSOLO: Ah Cécilia! Don't just stand there looking at people like an old witch surprised by daylight! Why don't you go and get something to eat for my sons? They can't drive all the way back to Yaoundé without eating anything!

(As CECILIA goes to the kitchen.)

Ah Tita-Mongô!

TITA-MONGO (running to the stage): O o o oh!

ABESSOLO: Help your uncle Mezôé take all these things to the house!

(Shaking a threatening fly-whisk at him.)

And don't you break any bottle, or I'll tan your hide!

(TITA-MONGO and MEZOE begin taking the cases to the main house.)

MEKA (delighted, stroking the things as they are being transported): Quite a lot of things! . . . Two cases of wine, four demijohns of . . . yes! . . . Red wine! . . . three cases of beer, meat, fresh and dried fish . . .

(Clapping his hands in admiration.)

Aa ah keeaah! There never was such an obedient daughter as our Matalina!

ADA (anxiously, taking some food to the kitchen): Will they be coming to see us at all?

MEZOE (taking more bottles to the main ohuse): The letter from the great man says: 'Until further notice . . . '

ADA (firmly): Then I'll go to Yaoundé and see them myself!

MEKA (to ADA who is going to the kitchen): Will you be the only one to do so, my daughter? Now that Matalina has married the man who rules everybody, where do you think this whole village will be going to spend a few months now and then, and eat vitamins with seven forks?

NKATEFOE: A very obedient daughter! She never missed a . . .

MEKA: Very obedient! She must have said to her husband: 'Since we aren't

Until Further Notice

going to Mvoutessi why not at least send one or two demijohns of red wine, and some meat, to the poor people who used to give me kilogrammes of cocoa whenever I was going to say good-bye to them before going back to school?'

ABESSOLO: She's a good daughter: she'll make us all very welcome . . .

(To the DRIVER and his COMPANION.)

Come, my sons! Let's go to the hall and sit down . . . This village is your village.

NKATEFOE (as they all go in): I think I'll be going back now . . . I haven't prepared my sermon for tomorrow morning yet.

(He picks up his Bible and hymnals from the small table.)

Since Matalina and her husband aren't coming . . .

ABESSOLO (sitting down): They can't come! My son-in-law himself sent me a letter . . . A letter in an envelope . . . They can't come, but we'll have a great dance here tonight. This whole village will come and eat and dr . . .

(Suddenly recollecting.)

Yes, of course! Your God doesn't drink!

NKATEFOE: I'll bring Odilia. We'll just come to eat the food.

ABESSOLO: Yes, come, and bring your wife.

(Sympathetically.)

Poor Nkatefoé! How many times have I told you to change your faith! Your God has too many taboos! Now that everything's changing, you must change too!

NKATEFOE (horrified): Me, change? You want me to go to the same heaven as a Catholic? Never!

(Going away.)

I'll bring Odilia . . . we'll just come to eat the food.

ABESSOLO: This whole village will come too.

(To MEZOE.)

Ah Mezôé! Go and read the letter from the city to Mbarga, the Chief himself. Ask him to come to our house tonight, he and all his wives. And don't forget to take a case of beer to him: you know how he always is . . .

MEZOE: Yes, Tita!

(He goes out to load the beer on his motorcycle.)

ABESSOLO: Ah Meka! You'd better go and beat my big talking drum behind the house, to ask everybody to come here tonight.

(As MEKA is going out.)

Until Further Notice

Wait! . . . Tell them also that Matalina and her husband won't be coming until . . .

(Shouting to MEZOE who is now starting his moped.)

Ah Mezoe! What did the letter say?

MEZOE (off stage): 'Until further notice . . . '

(He starts his moped, and goes away.)

ABESSOLO (to MEKA): Yes . . . until further notice. You tell them that. But don't forget to mention that they sent us lots of food and drinks. We'll have a big dance here tonight because our son-in-law has just been appointed a great man. Go and beat the talking drum, Meka!

THE DRIVER (as MEKA is going out): I daresay my father has been lucky in his old age!

ABESSOLO (with a self-satisifed sneer): How do I know, my son? We'll have to wait and see. Just because you hear the noise an elephant is making in the forest doesn't mean you've seen the elephant itself!

(He gets up.)

But let me help you with a drop of my own palm-wine.

(He goes to the far corner of the hall, and picks up one of the calabashes. He then begins filling up three tumblers while triumphantly muttering to himself.)

I knew Matalina would make her husband change his mind! . . . Things have changed! . . .

(With unconcealed pride as he remembers better days.)

And so have men!

(Coming back to the VISITORS.)

There you are, my sons: the best palm wine in the whole Fông region!

(The men start drinking; ABESSOLO sits down and carries on.)

There! Your old mother in the kitchen will soon bring you something nice to eat before you drive back.

(Playfully, leaning forward.)

But I'd better warn you: a hot, very hot dish! If you don't watch out, you'll be going back to the city with your tongues all burned and numb!

(The three of them burst out laughing heartily. Their laughter is soon covered by MEKA's enthusiastic message on the talking drum, and the curtain falls a few moments later.)

The Death of Chaka

AUTHOR'S PREFACE

On the eve of the white man's arrival, part of South Africa was dominated by a man belonging to a small African tribe. This man, Chaka, is today regarded by historians as one of the greatest military leaders of the past. 'A military genius consumed by an insatiable thirst for blood,' is the way his contemporaries, terrorized by the sound of his war-drums, spoke of him. In the eyes of history, Chaka is the greatest black conqueror to come out of Africa. At the height of his reign, his army, organized, disciplined and living in barracks, was estimated to number 400,000 men. This play is based on one of the accounts of his end.

CHARACTERS

CHAKA King of the Amazulu

DINGANA
MHLANGANA } his half-brothers, generals in the Zulu army

MAPO
UMSELE } generals in the Zulu army
MYOZI

NDLEBE
ISANUSI } confidants of Chaka

NOTIBE Mapo's sister, Dingana's fiancée

GENERALS

YOUNG WARRIORS

YOUNG WOMEN

The action of the play takes place in what is now Natal, South Africa, in 1828.

FIRST TABLEAU

Dingana's kraal, where the Generals are meeting

DINGANA: My friends, after the extermination of the
Amaqwabe and the Amachuna, we met in this same place
and each of us expressed his anxiety about Chaka's
military ambitions. Our discussion led us to review the
wider problems posed by Chaka's reign: the massacres
and burning of villages that he obliges us to carry out.
Unfortunately those discussions were too brief and we
were unable to make any decisions. Since then things
have gone on as before. Our own people have been
massacred. Beyond our borders we have massacred not
only our enemies, but even people who sought to do us
no harm. We have uprooted whole tribes. Today our
country covers an area which we ourselves cannot visua-
lize. I sincerely believed that now we would stop. But
I have just seen Chaka: he is planning another campaign.
This time it is to be against a powerful coalition of all the
tribes we have not yet exterminated but who live in a state
of fear and anxiety. They have assembled their forces
in the south and told Chaka that we are to regard the
mountains in the north as the limit of our territory and,
in the south, not to advance further than the Umfolozi
River. As could be expected, Chaka has refused. I think
we could negotiate. At all costs, we must persuade Chaka
to accept peace. If necessary, he must agree to surrender
part of our territory. Otherwise we will die on the battlefield and in poverty. We have won several victories.
Chaka must now leave us free to enjoy the vast wealth
we have accumulated. He must allow us to marry.

I know you agree with me. We have been muttering our discontent long enough. It seems to me that the time has come for us to have it out with Chaka. He must be made to understand that he cannot manage without us. After all, we have been his companions since the beginning and he owes much of his glory to us. So it is up to us to bring things to a head.

A silence

MHLANGANA (*laying his spear on a cowhide in the centre of the stage and returning to his place*): I am particularly grateful for the opportunity Dingana has given us today to talk things over. I see the problem a little differently. It seems to me that by confronting Chaka and telling him what we think we shall achieve little, except to be put to death. I know Chaka as well as you do. He is the child of war: blood, destruction, glory—these are what his life is made of. Think back to the time when Chaka was a child. Remember how, all alone, with only a stick, he routed a band of warriors armed with deadly spears. Remember how, on the battlefield, his face would shine for joy at the approach of the enemy, while everyone else was petrified with fear and choking with anxiety.

No, my friends. An interview with Chaka in the hopes of making him change his mind would only persuade him to execute us and he won't for a moment give up his plans for war. It seems to me we must face the facts. The beads and the cattle we have accumulated will be of no use to us as long as Chaka is our ruler. The people will have no respite. We must get rid of Chaka. That is the real problem. Don't be afraid of the facts. It may well be that Chaka cannot do without us, but this will in no way prevent him from having us executed in public. After Zwide and Batiwane had been crushed, anyone else but Chaka would have stopped. But for him it was only a beginning. You know what he is like. Nothing can stop him, nothing can make him change his mind. The greatness and the power of the Zulu people, the people of the sky, come first. Only Chaka, invested by Nkulunkulu, the Almighty, with the sacred mission of leading his people, may make decisions, give orders and command. Chaka alone rules. Only Chaka counts. Don't forget how he has just humiliated us. From now on no general will command his own *impi*. The warriors on one side, the generals on the other. When a battle is announced, Chaka will summon us and tell us which *impis* we are to command. The generals and the men won't know one another. No, my friends; it is Chaka who is the root of the problem.

Mhlangana takes up his spear. Murmurs

MAPO (*laying down his spear*): My friends, I've heard what has been said and reflected on it. It is quite true that we have often muttered against Chaka's errors. We've left behind us a trail of blood, too much blood. Chaka always expects a man to give more than he is able. I admit this. But as Mhlangana has just said, let's think back. What were we before Chaka? A host of weak tribes dominated by our neighbours. If one of them felt the urge to do so, he would swoop down upon us, carrying off our women, children and cattle, burning our homes, and then departing, leaving behind weeping and smouldering villages, terror and desolation. Remember how, at night, the wild animals would enter our villages with impunity, carrying off animals and children. We paid tribute to all our neighbours, and yet none spared us. It was in this atmosphere that Chaka was born. Today we are feared by everyone. It is to us that tribute is paid. Our villages now have warriors to protect them. Our women and children no longer fear marauders and wild

animals at night. Chaka has given our people a new
name, to ensure that they will always have confidence in
their destiny: *Amazulu*, the children of the sky. This
name alone makes our enemies tremble. Chaka has taught
both our generals and our warriors the art of war. Is there
any need to labour this point? Chaka has one virtue
which we are bound to recognize: he has never considered
himself too great for us. If anyone has a fever, Chaka
visits him. If a child is ill, Chaka sends for him and has
him cared for by his own healers. Chaka makes mistakes,
goes too far. This is true, but who among us ever told
him so? In fact, it is we who are to blame. None of us
ever dares to risk annoying Chaka by saying: this will not
do! Our sole thought has been for our positions, and
we have left him in isolation. We have often praised his
deeds when in fact we didn't approve of them. Now,
without first trying to have it out with him, we want to
get rid of him. No, I agree with Dingana. Let's see him.
If he puts us to death, it will be for the sake of the Zulu
people. If he lets us live and doesn't change his methods,
we'll have the courage to return our spears, which are the
emblems of our authority.

MHLANGANA: No! No! You cannot tell Chaka anything.
He doesn't like the truth. What he likes are our approval
and our praises. If we tell him what we want to tell him,
we'll immediately be accused of being his enemies.

MAPO: That's not true. Chaka is not like that. It is up to
you who are nearest to him to speak to him. If you are
weary, give up your spears. But don't betray both the
Zulu people and Chaka.

MHLANGANA: You are mad!

MAPO: Are you jealous of Chaka?

DINGANA: Come, come, friends. Let's hear what the others
have to say.

First Tableau

UMSELE: I think we should see him and speak to him. But we'll form ourselves into two groups. As a precaution, only the first group, of which I ask to be a member, will see him. If he puts us to death, the second group will then be able to deal with him.

MYOZI: It's a waste of time seeing him. If he doesn't put us to death, he'll remove us from our posts, turn the people against us, and then we'll no longer be able to do anything. Or, if we must speak to him, let's wait until this campaign is over. Then, if we win, we'll be in a stronger position to talk to him.

MHLANGANA: In my view, it's this war that we must avoid. The armies opposing us are too strong. The enemy outnumber us three to one.

MYOZI: Is that true? All the southern armies?

DINGANA: Yes, I'm afraid so. Our people could be destroyed.

Enter Notibe. She claps her hands

NOTIBE: I salute you, my elders.

A VOICE: Why have you come here?

NOTIBE: I am your sister. I am always ready to serve you. May I speak to you?

MAPO: No! No! Don't interfere, Notibe.

Protests from all sides

MYOZI: Friends, let her speak. Much can be learnt from women. Speak Notibe.

NOTIBE: I have overheard everything. There has been talk of bloodshed. Blood has indeed been spilt. There has been talk of violence, abuses, excesses. All this is perfectly true. There has been a lot of blood spilt in our path since Chaka's reign began. The blood of our enemies, the blood of our own people. Blood has been spilt on the battlefield and in our own villages. But for all that, you cannot desert Chaka. If he is doing wrong, go to him and tell him so. He may not be pleased to hear you tell him the truth, but if what you say is really true, he will in the end admit it.

A VOICE: And if he kills us?

NOTIBE: He can't kill everyone. Even if he kills two or three, he will in the end understand that killing isn't always the best solution. I know that going to Chaka with an opinion contrary to his own is very dangerous. But I also know that you are not afraid of death. You face it every day on the battlefield for Chaka and the Zulu people. Tell him the truth. Say no, for his sake and for the sake of us all. As men, that is your role. But don't forsake him, don't murder him.

A VOICE: Who said anything about murder?

NOTIBE: Let's be fair. Before Chaka neither our harvests nor our children belonged to us. We were the playthings of others. We were a laughing-stock. We were pillaged and massacred. In short, we were an enslaved people. And don't forget, I owe him a personal debt. I was that young girl who was carried off from a hut one night by a hyena. It was dark. I screamed and screamed. It was the time of the great terror. Everyone had shut himself in, trembling, and none dared venture outside. That night, for the first time, a young man dared confront the dreaded hyena. That young man was Chaka. He killed the beast and saved my life. And remember, too, how, during the same period, he faced a lion alone and killed it. Thanks to Chaka, the wild animals left us in peace, and men went down on their knees before him. All that needed blood-shed. But before Chaka, it was only our blood that was spilt, and it was shed with impunity. We lived in fear and famine. Such a man does not deserve to be betrayed by his own people. We would be cursed by Nkulunkulu. That is what I wanted to tell you. I am your sister, ready

---

to serve you. I bring you water when you are thirsty,
I bring you food when you ask for it. I cannot be anything
but what you want me to be. I compose praises in your
honour and I sing them. I am the first to be proud of your
exploits, but at the same time, if people speak ill of you,
I am the first to suffer. It is all this that makes me beg you
on my knees to think carefully. If today something
happens between you and Chaka, everyone will suffer
from it. If today you forsake Chaka, tomorrow's songs
will tell of it to our children. Your names will be passed
on from generation to generation. What I say about
Chaka is what all the people say about him. It is not
therefore the leader I am defending. It is because I want
to be able to be proud of you, to be able always to carry
my head high among my companions. It is for your
sakes that I speak. (*She clasps her hands.*) For you alone.

DINGANA: Notibe, you have said much. You are our sister,
but there are matters that women cannot understand.
But rest assured, we'll do nothing to bring ourselves into
dishonour. We are thinking of all our people, and we are
thinking of those who will come after us. It is the happiness of the whole people that concerns us. We aren't
afraid of approaching Chaka and talking to him.
If any of us thinks that Chaka is likely to put us to death,
and if the thought of this makes him hesitate, it isn't,
as you well know, out of fear of death. It is because we
too don't want it to be said in years to come that we
killed one another. Each one of us here recognizes Chaka's
achievements, and we are only seeking to improve them.
You can rest assured of this. Go, leave us.

Exit Notibe

A VOICE: Listen! The horns.

MAPO: It's the fall-in!

DINGANA: Yes! It is the fall-in!

The Death of Chaka

Suddenly a warrior enters. He goes up to Dingana
and strikes the ground with his spear

WARRIOR: Dingana, Chaka wants you to warn the generals.
The warriors have been told. We leave in a few moments.
Chaka thinks we should go out to meet the enemy and
destroy them on their own ground before they can march
on us. He himself will lead half the Machaka *impi*.
You will lead the *Black Shields*, Mhlangana will command
the *Bees*, Mapo one half of the *Red Shields* and Umsele
the other half. Myozi will lead the *Spearsmen impi*.
The other generals will be given their commands when
we reach the Red Mountains. Chaka thinks that is where
the battle should take place. So we must get there first.

Murmurs and protests from all sides.
Exit warrior. A silence

DINGANA: Friends, you have heard Chaka's message.
He'd told me the departure could be for today or tomorrow. I see he has decided on today.

A VOICE: But it means at least eight days' march!

Protests

DINGANA: Almost.

Murmurs

MHLANGANA: So, once again we are setting out because
Chaka wants it so. For Chaka's glory. Friends, it seems
to me the time has come to make our protest. Chaka
cannot lead several *impis* by himself. He will ask the
the reasons for our refusal, and this will give us the
opportunity to have it out with him.

DINGANA: No! That is a clumsy way of going about it,
and could lead to further trouble. If we refuse to set out,
Chaka will turn the people against us.

MHLANGANA: And so?

DINGANA: We would be killed and Chaka would remain
exactly as before. Chaka knows his people well. He will

stand his ground against the enemy and would be quite capable of defeating them, for every Zulu would become a soldier. We would be regarded as traitors.

A VOICE: You are right!

MHLANGANA: What do you suggest we do?

DINGANA: It would be wiser to go out and meet the enemy. When we are far from our villages, on foreign territory, we will be in a stronger position to speak to Chaka. It is easier for him to defend himself alone here, than to take on single-handed an enemy three times more numerous than we are and, what is more, on enemy territory.

Cries of approval

A VOICE: You are quite right!

DINGANA: I suggest we set out as soon as possible.

He rises. The others follow suit.

Curtain

SECOND TABLEAU

A wild part of the mountains.
Dingana, Mhlangana, Mapo

DINGANA: It has been left to us to decide. We have the confidence of all the generals. They are letting us act in their name. They will agree to whatever we decide. It is a heavy responsibility for us. What do you think we should do?

MAPO: Dingana, you are the wisest among us. You make your suggestions. Don't you agree, Mhlangana?

MHLANGANA: Yes, I do. I would also add that we have very little time. We must make up our minds quickly.

DINGANA: After five days' march we have now reached the gorges of the Red Mountains. It is here that, along with all those who support us, we were to have made our decision. But on the way the others appointed us to act in their name. Should we see Chaka? On reflection, I think no good can come of a discussion with him. We are in a strong position. Chaka, as we know him only too well, will want to fight tomorrow. We must prevent this. We have good reasons. After five days' march, the warriors are exhausted. The enemy are fresh and alert. They will overcome us. That is what we must tell him. We cannot think of fighting for at least eight days. In the meantime, we'll try and make contact with the enemy leaders. Our enemy is no longer facing us; he is in our midst. Our enemy is Chaka. On the way here he has put to death two of our closest companions, Nongogo and Mnyamane. We have had enough. He is no longer in his right mind. If you take my advice, then, we'll refuse to fight for eight days. In the meantime, we'll negotiate with the enemy. The plan will be to allow ourselves to be defeated and let Chaka fall into their hands.

MHLANGANA: I agree with you. I'm pleased to hear you say that the enemy is in our midst and that it is Chaka who is our real enemy. Anyone who can't see this is forgetting all that has happened and is deliberately blinding himself to what is happening every day. We shall never have peace with Chaka because everywhere we have spread ruin, desolation and death. We have wiped whole tribes from the face of the earth. Look what has happened to the Amaqwabe, the Butelezi and the Tembus. And what about the Amachunu and the Buya people? And these aren't the only ones. Can we forget how our own brothers have been put to death? The orgy is at its height. Chaka raises his assegai and points it to the skies. Those who dance badly are killed. Those who don't sing are killed. The warriors who return from the battlefield without their assegais are killed. Those who return with their assegais, but without an enemy assegai as well, are killed. And what sort of a life do we lead? No! We have taken a long time to make up our minds. Now, let us hesitate no longer.

MAPO: Dingana has said something which makes me think. Perhaps Chaka is no longer in his right mind. We might well think this is so after the murder of our two companions, Nongogo and Mnyamane. What had they done? None of us knows. Did they speak? Were they slandered? There are no answers to these questions. For my part, I am still in favour of having it out with him. I think we must try to find out what is really happening in Chaka's mind and heart. If he puts us to death, the others will still be there. In any case, I also know that the warriors won't be fit to fight for at least two days. I am undecided. What should we do?

The Death of Chaka

DINGANA: Mapo, believe me, Chaka really is going out of his mind. What he has achieved must be saved before it is destroyed. I understand your indecision, but time is short. If we don't do something now, we'll soon be on the brink of disaster.

MAPO: Decide!

Enter Ndlebe. Surprise

NDLEBE: In Chaka's name, I salute you!

DINGANA: What is it?

NDLEBE: Chaka has sent me. We meet the enemy at dawn.

Dingana leaps up. The three generals
exchange glances

DINGANA: I don't think it is either prudent or wise to go into battle immediately. In fact, I think it is almost impossible. After the long march of the last few days, the warriors are exhausted, their feet are swollen. They can't do any more. In my opinion, Chaka should wait eight days or so to allow every man to recover his strength. What do you think?

MHLANGANA: It is also my opinion. It seems to me that to fight straight away would be to invite defeat. The enemy are on their home ground, well fed, fresh and alert. They have an indisputable advantage over us. On our side, everyone is tired.

NDLEBE: I don't agree with you. It seems to me, on the contrary, that by fighting immediately we will retain our advantage by taking the enemy by surprise, whereas if we are foolish enough to wait, the enemy will have time to organize and prepare themselves. We would then be repulsed. Don't forget, they are on their home ground. In any case, our supplies won't last eight days, while the enemy have everything they need at hand. What would be the use of our march if we were to lose eight days by waiting?

MAPO: If we don't allow the warriors time to rest, we will be crushed. It is quite clear you do not realize the condi-

Second Tableau

tion of the warriors.

NDLEBE: I most certainly do. I am one of them myself. I am certain they will be in favour of fighting without delay and getting it over with.

DINGANA: You may not be tired, Ndlebe, but the others are. The generals are worried.

NDLEBE: Have you asked them all? Admit that it is you who want to rest.

MAPO: We don't need to ask them to see that they are exhausted.

MHLANGANA: Our reply to Chaka is that the army is not in a fit state to attack.

NDLEBE: I think we should tell Chaka the truth. It's not the men that are tired, but the generals. They have been that way for a long time now. I observe, I know how to keep my eyes open, but I also know that one has to keep quiet about many things.

MHLANGANA: We are indeed tired, and have been for some time. We are tired of wars that never end. We are tired of endless marches. We are tired of destruction. What is the purpose of it all? We began with forty or so villages. Now we have thousands. Isn't that enough? Are we going to spend all our life conquering and destroying? That's not what we want. We have fought all the wars we need to fight. We have had enough. We want to live in peace. We have so much cattle, we don't know what to do with it. We have plenty of land. What more do we need? We just don't understand. Each one of us has tried to find an answer. But this isn't the immediate problem. We tell you that the warriors are exhausted. If we fight today we will most certainly be wiped out.

NDLEBE: You must have a very narrow view of what is involved to talk like that. Have you forgotten what we were before? Why do we fight? We fight for the greatness

The Death of Chaka

of our country and for the future of our people. We don't fight for cattle, even less for beads. A few years ago we were a laughing-stock. Today we are all fully aware of the position we occupy. You can't achieve this by resting nor by peace. And we continue to fight to consolidate what we have won. That is our life.

MHLANGANA: No! I'll tell you what the truth really is. We fight for the sake of one man's prestige. We go on fighting for him to be able to enjoy the praise songs of the warriors and to make sure he has a place in tomorrow's legend. This is what we have realized, and that is why, as you say, we have been weary for a long time now.

NDLEBE: What you say is unjust. It is for the honour and the greatness of the Zulu people that you go on fighting. Look at Chaka. He is the first to set an example. He accompanies you onto the battlefield. He shares your life in the barracks. He accompanies you in your training. He submits himself to the same hardships as you, to the same sacrifices. It is unjust and false to say that you fight for the glory of one man. You fight for yourselves.

MHLANGANA: One only fights to enjoy the fruits of victory. I said a moment ago: now we have cattle, but they are worthless to us. We have beads, but we make no use of them. None of us has a decent home. We are not even allowed to marry. And all for what? Will you tell me? Explain it to me. I can't understand.

NDLEBE: You must make your choice: indolence and pleasure or greatness. The tribes you have defeated, the peoples you have conquered all lived the kind of life to which you aspire. These men indulged freely in pleasure and in idleness, and that is why they were defeated. Surely you realize the need to deprive yourselves so that those who come after you can enjoy the fruits of your achievements? It will be for your children and grandchildren. But this will only be possible when, by your battles and your victories, you have eliminated every danger. For my part, I am proud to be a Zulu at this time. And I am sure that every warrior feels just as I do. The glory of my people is sung by other peoples. Formerly a laughing-stock, my people are now feared by everyone. Our wives are proud to compose praise songs in honour of their husbands. Before, they lived in terror; before, nothing belonged to them, neither their children nor their husbands. The neighbouring tribes were constantly carrying off men and cattle, leaving behind them desolation and fear. Even if I die in poverty, I know I have not lived for nothing. In all honesty I tell you, until the end of my life I will salute Chaka. If we are what we are, it is because we have had a leader who knew how to organize us, who knew how to guide us, who knew how to give the whole people that confidence without which there can be no victories. Cattle don't interest me. Cattle can die from sickness, cattle can be attacked and destroyed by wild animals. Beads don't interest me; they can be stolen. But the pride I bear with me today belongs to me. No one can take it from me.

DINGANA: Ndlebe, some men can live on wind. Others need meat. Some men can work to satisfy their thirst for greatness. Others are only happy when they have beads in their hands or on their foreheads. Of these, those who talk of greatness, honour and prestige are not far from madness. Let us not forget that man is a creature of flesh and blood.

NDLEBE: I am quite willing to be counted among the madmen who believe in their country, who believe in their leader, especially when this leader has never done anything for himself and devotes himself entirely to his country. Madmen like these are necessary to enable those who want meat and beads to live. The hyena also wants meat.

The Death of Chaka

It finds it where it can. It slinks on its belly to get it; it walks in the dark, fleeing the light, fleeing anything that makes it visible, solely to have meat. I myself will never eat that kind of meat, for one has to eat it with bowed head. Chaka has done everything for you. He has made you what you are, and this is what you think of your leader, your guide and your people.

DINGANA: And us? Haven't we done anything for Chaka? The victories we have won, who were they for?

NDLEBE: Who taught you to fight, to hold the assegai? Who taught you to lead men? Wasn't it Chaka? He is not a leader who stays in the shade while the others are out in the sun. All the great victories were won by him. Have you forgotten that first battle, when he faced Zwide's forty thousand men with an army of twenty thousand? Have you forgotten how Batiwane and the Butelezi were crushed?

MHLANGANA: That's right. Nothing but praise for Chaka. It is you and one or two others who live in his shadow, his confidants, who put such ideas into his head. It is you who are to blame.

NDLEBE: I accept that. I am not in the least ashamed to serve Chaka. He is better than any of us. It is precisely because I am devoted to my people, to the happiness of my people, that I serve Chaka faithfully. I have never asked for anything else, neither beads nor cattle, and I have taken part in all the campaigns myself, armed with my assegai. But the rest of you are little men. Let me tell you. You think obedience lowers you. You are mistaken. Obedience lowers no one; on the contrary, it makes you great.

MHLANGANA: You are a servant. We have a different idea of ourselves. Chaka destroys everything he creates. Our closest companions leave us and flee or are put to death. Where are Msilikazi and Manukusa? They have fled with their *impis*. They couldn't take any more. As for

Second Tableau

Nongogo and Mnyamane, they have been killed. Whose is the greatness you talk about? Chaka, Chaka alone is great. Whose is the glory? Chaka's. The glory is his alone.

DINGANA: We have said enough, I think. We have expressed ourselves fully and frankly. The one good thing, you see, Ndlebe, is that, whatever the bitterness some of us may feel, we know that Chaka is our brother and our leader. All we want is for everyone to be happy. But it is difficult to reach agreement on this subject. We are now going to see the others. I think Chaka will agree to grant just two days' rest to the warriors. This is what we'll propose. Wait here for our reply, and you'll soon learn that all the generals think the warriors need eight days' rest before we undertake any offensive.

Ndlebe does not reply, but remains seated,
his head between his hands.
Enter Notibe. She goes up to Ndlebe

NOTIBE: Ndlebe, I overheard everything. I'm disappointed. I had believed until now that we had men and leaders who, with Chaka, could lead our people to a great destiny. Now I'm in despair and afraid. What will become of our people after Chaka? I feel that we'll become even more insignificant than before. We'll be broken up and scattered. It is sad to think of it. And now, at the gates of the enemy, what is going to happen?

NDLEBE: I, too, am thinking about all these things. But there is no need to worry about the way things are at present. I have confidence in Chaka. It was he who made these men what they are. It was he who taught them the art of war. Perhaps when they're alone together again they'll forget all they've just said to me. As for our people's future, I'm not worried. The seeds sown by Chaka will germinate in a few minds. The men you have just seen are morally no longer with us. They are seeking something else. What we must hope for now is that they will not desert Chaka at the very gates of the enemy.

NOTIBE: You think they could change their minds when they find themselves face to face with Chaka?

NDLEBE: I hope so. But I am fully aware that one of the emotions prompting them today is jealousy. They are afraid of Chaka, certainly; but they are also jealous of him. They think that by opposing Chaka they are asserting themselves. As far as they are concerned, neither their country nor their people exist, and that is what is really disturbing about it all. You heard them, didn't you? They accuse me and everyone around Chaka. Why? Because they regard us as obstacles in the way of their ambitions. If they cannot manage to deceive Chaka, if they cannot manage to satisfy their ambitions, we are to blame. There is nothing new about this kind of attitude.

NOTIBE: I was Mapo's sister. I was Dingana's fiancée. Now, I am neither Mapo's sister nor Dingana's fiancée. I am Chaka's daughter. Like everyone else, I am a Zulu, and like many of the young people, I cannot live if Chaka dies. If my people must collapse, I prefer to be dead and buried.

Noises are heard off-stage. Exit Notibe
running. Enter Dingana

DINGANA: Ndlebe, the generals ask for three days. They are firm about this. At all costs they want to avoid leading the soldiers, in their present state of exhaustion, to death and defeat.

NDLEBE (*rising*): I shall go at once and inform Chaka of their decision. But before I go, let me say that the responsibility for the disaster will be on the heads of the men who had the confidence of the people and were entrusted with their destiny.

Curtain

THIRD TABLEAU

Chaka, Isanusi

CHAKA: You know, Isanusi, something strange is happening to me. For several days I have felt strangely weary and sick at heart. I have never felt like this before. I wanted you, who know so many things, and who know me so well, to come and tell me what is the matter with me. You and Ndlebe are the only two people of whom I can ask this kind of question.

ISANUSI: What is the cause of this weariness, Chaka? Think how far you have come. Do you remember our first meeting? You were lost in the forest and you were tired. You were asleep, still holding your assegai. I watched you for a long time and I saw your remarkable destiny written in your face. With Ndlebe, I put myself at your service, without reserve, without any thought of gain, simply and always with the pride of sharing in a great work. You were homeless, persecuted by your brothers and the members of your age group. Now, you have the world at your feet. You started from the village of Qwobe and now you rule all the villages in the land. From a host of tribes living in anarchy and unconcerned about their future, you have made a great people conscious of its greatness and ready to make any sacrifice to retain it. You have turned undisciplined, aimless warriors into fearless soldiers, handling the assegai as never before. A new people has been born, thanks to your faith and your genius—the *Amazulu*, the children of the sky. It was to achieve this that Nkulunkulu, the Almighty, sent you. Your work has been accomplished, and so, too, has your destiny.

Enter Ndlebe

NDLEBE: Bayete, Chaka!

CHAKA: Greetings, Ndlebe. Are the generals ready to attack at dawn?

Ndlebe remains silent and shakes his head

CHAKA: What is wrong? Speak!

NDLEBE: I don't know how to explain what I have to tell you, but we must abandon the plan to attack the enemy at dawn.

ISANUSI: Why?

NDLEBE: The generals are troubled, Chaka. They say the warriors are tired. The generals themselves are tired. They're not prepared to go into battle. None of my arguments could make them forget their tiredness.

CHAKA: If it is at the very gates of the enemy that the generals say they are tired, I shall put them to death.

NDLEBE: And who will command the *impis*?

CHAKA: Chaka will conduct the war alone, Chaka and two young officers. I had already foreseen this some time ago. There will be three *impis*: Chaka in the centre, at the advance tip, and the other two on each flank, slightly in arrear. When the enemy know—and we shall make sure they do—that Chaka is at the head, they'll send all their forces against him so as to capture him alive. Chaka will retreat to allow them to penetrate further between the two *impis*. In this way, they will be surrounded.

ISANUSI: These tactics seem excellent to me.

NDLEBE: But couldn't you first try and persuade the generals to change their minds?

CHAKA: If you really want me to. But you know how tired they are! (*with irony*)

NDLEBE: In that case, Chaka, I advise you not to put them

Third Tableau

to death. Fight on your own, fight with those who are willing. Let the generals rest, and let them enjoy the fruits of their victory all the same. Spare their lives. Perhaps they are expecting you to put them to death. On no account must you confront them, because if you do you will lose the battle. The enemy will no longer be afraid of our men if we kill one another, and the people will begin to ask questions. When a man is a leader of men, it must not be possible to say of him all the time: if we do this, he will do that. It's a good thing for a leader to have an air of mystery, something unknown about him.

CHAKA (*raising his hand*): Ndlebe, I know the generals aren't with me. For some time now this knowledge has weighed heavily upon me. The generals wish for pleasure, a life of ease and orgies; in short, a life which has nothing to do with fighting. That is why Msilikazi and Manukuza left. Others, like Nongogo and Mnyamane have wanted to take my life. I've had them put to death. I have always believed, and I still believe, in the destiny of my people. I, Chaka, have been the instrument of this destiny. We had a mission; Nkulunkulu, the Almighty, assigned us a task and it had to be accomplished. People say that I've left a trail of blood behind me: the blood of enemies, the blood of people who wished us no harm and, often, even the blood of friends. One thing I know: power is like a limpid, clear pool. You look at it, you see yourself reflected in it, and you admire its limpidity; but at the bottom of that pool, the sand is not always pure; it is often mixed with mud. Even here, among my own people, I have put to death the cowards and the waverers because, you see, man is an animal with two heads. One is named Greatness, the other Mediocrity. Greatness is born out of sacrifice and suffering. Mediocrity grows on idleness,

118

The Death of Chaka

indifference and pleasure. I wanted to cut this head from
my people, but it is difficult to overcome it. It is like the
mushrooms that spring up after the rain. But I know
Chaka will never die. A new generation of young men,
especially my own children, the Machaka, rise towards
the sun with the heart and mind of Chaka. Yes, with the
heart and mind of Chaka. They are always ready to
fight. I am going to speak to them straight away. Go,
Isanusi; call their captains.

Exit Isanusi

NDLEBE: Chaka, I am your friend. I am your brother.
I've always spoken my mind when you've sought my
advice, and often I've given you my opinion unsolicited.
I have never praised you. Today we are faced with a
situation that is quite different, a painful situation. I
have confidence in you. I have faith in you. I know you
will win. Bayete, Bayete, Chaka!

CHAKA: Thank you, Ndlebe. You are my friend and my
brother. What you say is true. Until you came, I never
realized I could be wrong. Those who surrounded me had
no truth but mine, no arguments but my arguments.
Those were weak men, little men. You disagreed with me,
and I admired you. You have had a great deal to do with
the fulfilling of my destiny. I thank you, Ndlebe.

*Enter seven young warriors carrying assegais. They
raise their assegais*

WARRIORS: Bayete, Chaka! Bayete, Baba! Bayete, Lord!
Bayete, Zulu!

*On a sign from Chaka, they fall on their
knees before him*

CHAKA: My children, we are about to fight our last battle.
All our enemies have united in coalition against us.
We will crush them, to establish, once and for all, the
greatness of our people. In this battle, each one of us must

fight like three warriors. The enemy are more numerous
than we are. But don't forget you are the sons of the sky.
We will form three *impis* only: yours, which I shall
lead personally, and two others led by Ndlebe and Isanusi.
In this way our forces will rout the enemy. This will be
the young men's battle. It will be the battle of destiny.
You will show whether you are able to bring to fruition
the field we have ploughed. The generals probably won't
take part. They will watch you in action, for tomorrow
it will be your duty to keep the wild animals from our
villages. You will carry the name of our people to even
further lands, lands which are still unknown to us. Are
you willing to die for the greatness and the honour of the
Zulu people?
The young warriors raise their assegais
WARRIORS: Bayete, Lord! Bayete, Chaka! Bayete, Zulu!
We promise to obey you, and if we do not win this battle,
we prefer to die. But we'll always try to obey you.
Sound of drums. The young warriors dance.

Curtain

FOURTH TABLEAU

Chaka, Ndlebe

CHAKA: Ndlebe, have you taken my message to the *impis*? You and Isanusi will lead your respective *impis*, with two young captains of the Machaka as your seconds-in-command. Chaka will be in the centre.

NDLEBE: I thought you should first speak to the generals.

CHAKA: You are right. Have you summoned them?

NDLEBE: Yes. They are coming. But Dingana's fiancée wants to speak to you first.

CHAKA: Where is she?

NDLEBE: She is outside. I'll send her in.

Exit Ndlebe. He returns, followed by a young girl.
She claps her hands and falls on her knees

NOTIBE: Bayete, Chaka! Bayete, Zulu!

CHAKA: What is it, Notibe?

NOTIBE: Chaka, I am troubled. I am full of anxiety. I feel we are threatened by danger. I wanted to see you to tell you what the women and young girls feel about you, to thank you for all that you have done for our people. Our mothers were the servants of other women. They carried water to other warriors. They washed their clothing, looked after their cattle. They composed the praises of others. But now, with you, Chaka, it is the warriors of other tribes who go on their knees before our mothers, who build our huts and take our cattle to graze. This is what the women sing of now, Chaka.

CHAKA: Where is the danger, my daughter? Don't you have confidence in your own people?

NOTIBE: Yes, Chaka, my lord; yes, I do. But I want you to

stay with us as long as possible, for the glory of my people.

CHAKA: Rest assured, my daughter. Henceforth Chakas will be born throughout the history of our people, for no other kind of man will be able to command the Zulus. Those who fail to see this are blind. You are a girl. Tomorrow you will relate the exploits of Chaka to your children. You will tell them that one day the Lord of the Deep Water said to Chaka, on the bank of a river: 'I will give you good fortune, I will give you cattle and I will give you glory in the midst of your people.' And Chaka asked: 'In the meanwhile what will become of my people?' The Lord of the Deep Water replied: 'Why concern yourself with others? They will live in misery.' And Chaka begged him: 'Grant me the greatness of my people and leave me in misery.' Then the Lord of the Deep Water said: 'Already you bear in you the greatness of your people. You will rule the rivers and the mountains; you will transform whole regions into paths to give you passage; the lions will roar forth your glory and the birds will sing the praises of your army.' That is what you will tell them, my daughter.

NOTIBE: Chaka, may you live forever! (*She rises.*) Today my happiness is complete. I have no more fear. Bayete, Lord! Bayete, Zulu! Bayete!

Exit.

After a few moments, enter the generals

GENERALS: Bayete! Bayete, Chaka!

They crouch down. For a while,
Chaka looks into their faces

CHAKA: I have decided to attack the enemy at dawn. What do you think?

A silence

DINGANA: Chaka, my lord, I think it would be better to wait a few days. The warriors are exhausted. As we've

The Death of Chaka

already told Ndlebe, many of them have swollen feet from the march we've just completed. We're not fit for battle.

MAPO: Yes, that is true. It would be better to wait a few days. We would then have time to prepare ourselves properly. What we want is a complete and total victory from which the enemy will never recover.

MHLANGANA: If we attack at dawn we risk defeat. The enemy is on his home ground, rested, well-fed, while, as for us, we... The soldiers are exhausted. They are hungry.

A silence

CHAKA: If I understand you properly, you want three days' rest? I will ask you a question: if the enemy were to attack us tomorrow, what would we do?

DINGANA (*after a moment's hesitation*); I don't think they will attack. The rapidity of our march has taken them by surprise.

MHLANGANA: They won't dare attack.

CHAKA: Can you see into their minds? Answer my question. What if they attack us? What will we do? If I follow you correctly, even if they did attack us, we would not fight?

DINGANA: My lord, we did not say that.

CHAKA: Answer then. What would we do if they attacked us?

MAPO: If we are forced to fight, we'll do so. But, I repeat, I don't think they will attack us.

CHAKA: In other words, if the enemy attack us, we'll fight all the same? Don't you see what will happen? We'll be on the defensive and we'll lose the advantage we have over them.

A silence

DINGANA: In any case, the warriors are tired. We must not court defeat.

CHAKA: I have understood you perfectly well. But I have

Fourth Tableau

come into the enemy's territory to fight, not to rest. The warriors, too, have come to fight. This is what they are waiting for. If we wait three days, we'll give the enemy time to prepare themselves. I cannot do this. The battle will take place at dawn. I have decided to go out to meet the enemy with three *impis* only. You will rest. I shall lead one of the *impis*. Isanusi and Ndlebe will lead the other two.

MHLANGANA: My lord, I feel you should not expose yourself any more. You mean too much to our people. Surely you are not going to match yourself against these men of no importance. Why don't you listen to us? All we want is to be the strongest every time. That is why we ask for three days.

CHAKA: You say the enemy are of no importance, yet you feel you need rest before confronting them. No. We attack at dawn, at no other time. I know you are tired. I can feel it. Let the young men show their worth, then. We'll see what they can do. The discussion is over, since I have to conduct the war. I am going to ask you to join me in dancing the dance of the *impis*. I suppose you can manage that? Then, when we return from the battle, we will rejoice together, you, the warriors and I. We'll be proud of our young men, and we'll know that after us the Zulu people will be greater than ever before!

He lifts his assegai, then rises. The drums beat. The dance begins, Chaka in front.

Curtain

FIFTH TABLEAU

Chaka, Ndlebe and Isanusi, beneath a tree

CHAKA: Ndlebe, did you lose many men?

NDLEBE: Yes, especially at the beginning. When we tried to envelop the enemy, we encountered unbelievable resistance. It came from a tribe equipped with strange shields, of a kind we had never seen before. Their warriors fought much as we do, that is, with short assegais, in hand to hand combat. Fortunately, thanks to you, we have a technique which no one else can equal. We were a little surprised by the enemy's fervour in battle. That was when we lost most of our men. But as soon as we had recovered ourselves, we routed them.

CHAKA: And you, Isanusi?

ISANUSI: I lost quite a few men, my lord. It wasn't because the enemy were better fighters, but because they were so numerous. It was ten to one. And you, Chaka?

CHAKA: No, not many. The Machaka followed my instructions scrupulously. At first, the enemy sent their best troops against us. There was disorder in their ranks when we retreated to draw them on. Some of them, believing we had already lost the battle, wanted to distinguish themselves and were too eager. We took advantage of this to engulf them. My Machaka are lions.

ISANUSI: What's strange is the disappearance of the enemy generals.

CHAKA: It's a well-known tactic. When the generals realize that the battle has been lost, they immediately get rid of everything that distinguishes them from their warriors: clothing, shield, assegai. They then look like everyone else. I expect they are among the prisoners. But that's of no importance. The enemy's army has been crushed and their whole territory is at our feet.

NDLEBE: What will you do now with our own generals, Chaka?

CHAKA: Nothing. They are no longer generals. Simple warriors are worth more than they are. I think if they have anything left of the Zulu in them, they will disappear of their own accord. But that's not what I was thinking about. I was telling Isanusi earlier that I felt weary and sick at heart. I feel it more than ever now. I am like the sun at the end of the day. I feel it. I think of my people. In spite of the victories, in spite of the glory and prestige associated with the name of Zulu, since the battle was over, I have had the feeling that a danger lies in wait for them. In a moment I'm going to speak to Nkulunkulu to discover what this danger is. But I think I already know what it is.

NDLEBE: Yet another danger, Chaka! Just when we're the masters of the world. We've subjected all the tribes. We've crushed all those who resisted us and exterminated those who were unwilling to accept our domination. What more do you want, Chaka? My lord, today you are the greatest general in the world. It is to you alone that the Almighty has taught the art of war. Victory is like your shadow; it follows you everywhere. You raise your assegai and victory flings itself into your arms. Bayete, Bayete, Lord! You are the sun. After one day, another day is yours. You will be with us as long as the sky is above our heads, as long as there is light in our eyes. Bayete, Chaka! You have just shown, once more, that you are greater than all the generals together.

A noise is heard in the wings. Enter young men and young women. The young women carry pots full of water. They

The Death of Chaka

go up to Chaka, who dips his hand in each pot. The young men are behind the young women and hold out their assegais to Chaka

YOUNG MEN AND YOUNG WOMEN: Bayete, Chaka! Bayete, Lord! Bayete, Baba! Oh Zulu! We thank you for this victory. We thank you for yet another victory. The people are proud of you, the people are full of joy. We salute you, son of the sky. We salute you, messenger of the Eternal, messenger of Nkulunkulu. The enemy are at our feet, their cattle belong to our people. Until the end of time, your praises will be sung by us, by all all those who come after us, by all those who know but one way, the way of honour and greatness! By all those who serve others and who serve the future. Bayete, Lord!

CHAKA: Thank you, my children. I wanted to speak to you, and I am pleased you have come. You have grown up with our people. You belong to the generation which has not known all that we suffered. You are the witnesses of our second life, and I want that life to be yours, so that it may be the only life that matters to you. Our people seem to me to be made for greatness because they know how to obey, because they know how to deprive themselves, because they have endurance. Soon our land will be in a state of turmoil. Something extraordinary is about to happen. There will be storms. For a while there will be no light, only torture and humiliation. But keep alive the memory of this victory and never forget how we won it. I repeat: we won it because we knew how to obey, because we knew what we wanted, because we were able to forget ourselves for the sake of a unity we believed greater than the individual. Believe me, whatever happens, you will have the foundations of the society we have already created to give you the light and guidance you will need in order to come through the long, long night we

Fifth Tableau

are about to enter. But I, Chaka, am convinced that, thanks to the virtues of my people, at the end of that night they will find a new dawn, a bright and spotless dawn which will shine with honour, dignity and glory. I salute you, my children. Always live for others.

YOUNG MEN AND YOUNG WOMEN: Bayete, Chaka! Bayete, Oh Baba! Bayete, Zulu, master of war!

Exeunt the young men and young women

CHAKA: Where are the generals?

NDLEBE: No one knows. They must be somewhere close by.

CHAKA: Now, my friends, leave me alone. I am going to offer my thanks once more to the Almighty for having granted my people yet another victory.

NDLEBE: Don't you want us to stay with you?

CHAKA: No. You know I never allow anyone to be present when I speak to our Master.

ISANUSI: But we aren't at home! We are in enemy territory!

CHAKA: You forget our victory. We are at home. We have beaten the enemy.

Exeunt Isanusi and Ndlebe. Chaka rises, stands motionless and extends his hands. He remains standing a moment, silent. Enter three men walking on the tips of their toes. The first goes up to Chaka and stabs him in the back with an assegai. The other two do the same. Chaka staggers and leans against the wall. He looks at them

CHAKA: You are murdering me so as to take my place. You are too late. Umlungu, the white man, is on his way. You will be his subjects.

He falls.

Curtain

Caraf Books
Caribbean and African Literature
Translated from French

Serious writing in French in the Caribbean and Africa has developed unique characteristics in this century. Colonialism was its crucible; African independence in the 1960s its liberating force. The struggles of nation-building and even the constraints of neocolonialism have marked the coming of age of literatures that now gradually distance themselves from the common matrix.

CARAF BOOKS is a collection of novels, plays, poetry, and essays from the regions of the Caribbean and the African continent that have shared this linguistic, cultural, and political heritage while working out their new identity against a background of conflict.

An original feature of the CARAF BOOKS collection is the substantial critical introduction in which a scholar who knows the literature well sets each book in its cultural context and makes it accessible to the student and the general reader.

Most of the books selected for the CARAF collection are being published in English for the first time; some are important books that have been out of print in English or were first issued in editions with a limited distribution. In all cases CARAF BOOKS offers the discerning reader new wine in new bottles.

The Editorial Board of CARAF BOOKS consists of A. James Arnold, University of Virginia, General Editor; Kandioura Dramé, University of Virginia, Associate Editor; and two Consulting Editors, Abiola Irele of the University of Ibadan, Nigeria, and J. Michael Dash of the University of the West Indies in Mona, Jamaica.

Guillaume Oyônô-Mbia and Sedlou Badian, *Faces of African
   Independence: Three Plays*
Olympe Bhêly-Quénum, *Snares without End*